MORE GREAT PANTYHOSE CRAFTS

A Family Workshop Book

MORE GREAT PANTYHOSE CRAFTS

by Ed & Stevie Baldwin

DOUBLEDAY & COMPANY, INC.
GARDEN CITY, NEW YORK
1984

Created by The Family Workshop, Inc.
Editorial Director: Janet Weberling
Editors: Suzi West, Mike McUsic, Rhonda Mulberry, Mary Milander
Art Director: Dale Crain
Production Artists: Wanda Young, Roberta Taff, Verna Stonecipher-Fuller,
                    Janice Harris Burstall, Paula Kempe, Eddy Simpson
Typography: Deborah Gahm
Creative Director: April Bail
Project Designs: April Bail, Stevie Baldwin, Janice McKinney, Tanya Cunningham
Photography: Bill Welch

The information in this book is correct and complete to the best of our knowledge. All recommendations are made without guarantees on the part of the authors or Doubleday & Company, Inc., who disclaim all liability in connection with the use of this information.

The Family Workshop's catalog of project plans is available for $2.95 from: The Family Workshop, Inc., P. O. Box 1000, Bixby, OK 74008

For Roger, Iola, Mel, Justin, and Sean.

Library of Congress Cataloging in Publication Data

Baldwin, Ed.
    More great pantyhose crafts.

    1. Pantyhose craft.   I. Baldwin, Stevie.   II. Title.
TT699.B337   1985   745.58′4
ISBN: 0-385-19934-1

Library of Congress Catalog Card Number 84–22282
Copyright © 1985 by The Family Workshop, Inc.
All Rights Reserved
Printed in the United States of America
First Edition

Preface

Before the invention of pantyhose, there were things called nylon stockings. Stockings were made as separate units, one for each leg. Pantyhose, on the other hand (or should we say, leg), aren't made that way. The individual units are combined, which means that a run in one pantyhose leg ruins the whole shebang. Are you going to throw away the pantyhose and feel like you've wasted money, or ignore the run and hope everyone else ignores it as well? Let's face it – neither option is golden.

Well, despair no longer! This book presents many original, beautiful, and creative craft projects that can be made from those almost-good pantyhose. We've included something for everyone in the family, from the purely whimsical to the perfectly practical.

Each project plan includes a complete materials list, step-by-step instructions, scale drawings or full-size patterns, and colorful assembly diagrams. There is a full-color photograph of each finished project to help you visualize what you're making.

The Tips & Techniques section provides information on materials, sewing procedures, soft-sculpting techniques, and many other helpful hints. We suggest that you read this section before beginning any of the projects.

We would like to offer special thanks to the Necchi Corporation, who provided the sewing machine we used to make the projects; and to Tanya Cunningham, who designed and made the adorable little bunny in our Easter Bunny Egg project.

We hope you will enjoy making the projects in this book as much as we did. Perhaps the next run in your pantyhose will seem less like a dead-end than a brand-new beginning!

Contents

Choosing Materials

Pantyhose are available in many colors, weights, and weaves. While heavier weights and weaves are sturdier, they are too firm to allow for easy soft-sculpting. Support-type hose should never be used, unless they are specifically called for in the instructions.

The type of pantyhose for each project is specified in the materials list for that project. When regular-weave pantyhose are specified, any flesh-colored hose (from light to dark) may be used. The instructions assume that the hose have a reinforced toe, heel, and panty. If you use sandal foot or sheer-to-the-waist hose, simply follow the instructions for cutting the hose as if the reinforced portions were there. When queen-size hose are specified, it is because of the size of the project and the resulting strain that is put on the hose. Regular (non-support) hose can be used instead of queen-size if you reduce the size of the finished project.

In most of the projects, we have specified the colors and types of fabric that we used. Choose fabric weights and finishes that are similar to those specified; fabric color, however, is always optional. Choose fabrics that suit your personal taste and color scheme. Always wash, dry, and press the fabrics before using.

We have specified heavy-duty thread for all sculpting, and for seams that will be taking an unusual amount of stress. The best thread for this purpose is 100 percent nylon with a bonded finish, usually sold for drapery making. It will take the strain without breaking, and is not apt to hurt your hands.

Tools of the Trade

A long sharp needle is best for sculpting. A "sharp" is a type of needle commonly available in fabric stores. Select a needle that is long enough to push through a stuffed pantyhose head without getting lost, but that is not so large that the eye of the needle makes holes (and resulting runs) in the hose. The needle should be fairly sturdy; not too flimsy or flexible.

Ordinary white glue can be used to make all of the projects in this book. Hot-melt adhesive, however, is a real timesaver. This glue comes in solid sticks that are inserted into a special glue gun. The gun heats the glue stick, and dispenses melted glue when you pull the trigger. The hot glue can be used to adhere fabric to hose, or hose to hose. It is a very quick process, and will eliminate the clamping time required for white glue. Hot-melt adhesive can also be used in many applications as a substitute for hand stitching.

The glue is extremely hot when it is ejected from the gun, and will blister your fingers if you touch it before it cools. For that reason, use great care when working with a glue gun. Surprisingly enough, the extremely hot glue will not melt the hose.

Enlarging Scale Drawings

Many of the large pattern pieces in this book are specified as scale drawings, which you will need to enlarge to full-size before cutting out the fabric. In order to do this, you will need pattern paper that contains a grid of 1-inch squares. You can purchase dressmaker's pattern paper which already has a grid on it or you can make your own using large sheets of tracing paper or brown wrapping paper.

Figure A

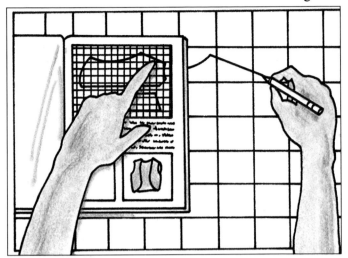

First, count the number of squares that the scale drawing occupies; since each square represents one inch, this will tell you how large a piece of paper you will need for the pattern. Next, draw horizontal and vertical lines that meet at a 90-degree angle. If this angle is not perfectly square, your grid will be made of "leaning inches"…great for a tower in Pisa, but not so good for patterns. Mark 1-inch increments along both lines, and draw additional lines across the marks using a straight edge or ruler…keep them square!

Place your homemade or purchased pattern paper on a flat surface. It is now simply a matter of reproducing the scale drawing onto the graph paper. The key is to duplicate the lines one square at a time (**Figure A**).

After you have enlarged the scale drawings into full-size patterns, transfer all of the sewing or cutting directions that appear on the drawing to the patterns. Be sure to mark the "place on fold" lines, so they won't be mistaken for cutting lines.

Some patterns in this book are provided full-size; these should first be transferred to pattern paper or tracing paper, and then cut out. This will save cutting up your book.

Sewing Definitions

Basting stitches are used to hold the fabric in place temporarily before the final stitching is done by hand or machine. They are also used to gather the fabric.

To baste, take long, running stitches through the fabric layers. Hand basting stitches are usually ½ inch in length. To baste by machine, simply set the stitch-length selector to the longest stitch available. For basting stitches that need to be removed, use a thread color that is easy to see (**Figure B**).

Topstitching is a final stitch on the right side of the fabric, and usually will show on the finished project. Topstitching should be very straight, and a uniform distance from the edge of the fabric (**Figure C**).

Figure B

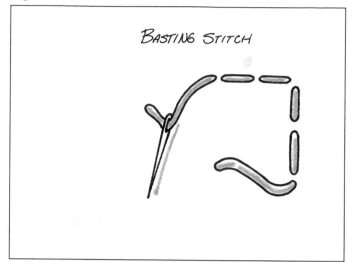

BASTING STITCH

Figure C

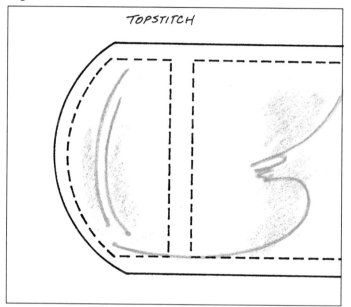

TOPSTITCH

Figure D

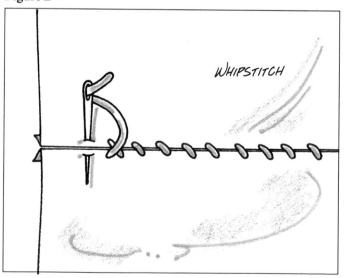

WHIPSTITCH

Figure E

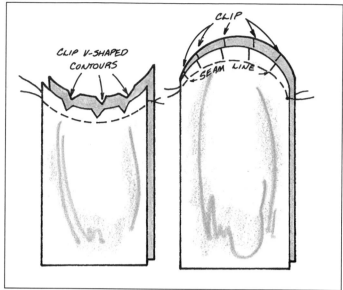

CLIP

CLIP V-SHAPED CONTOURS

SEAM LINE

Figure F

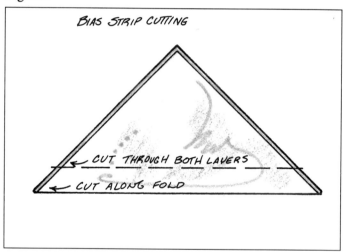

BIAS STRIP CUTTING

CUT THROUGH BOTH LAYERS

CUT ALONG FOLD

Whipstitching joins two fabric pieces together, catching an equal amount of fabric on each edge. Each stitch is worked straight across perpendicularly to the fabric edges, resulting in a diagonal stitch pattern on the visible side of the fabric, as shown in **Figure D**.

Clipping seams is necessary on curves or corners so the finished project will lie flat when turned and pressed. To eliminate excess seam allowance on an outward curve or corner, cut V-shaped notches in the seam allowance. Be careful not to cut through the seam stitches. Inside curves must also be clipped, since there will not be enough fabric in the seam allowance to turn the curve. Make straight clips toward the seam allowance and end your cut as close to the stitched seam as possible without cutting through it (**Figure E**).

Bias strips of fabric are cut so the grain runs diagonally. Fabric that is on the bias is stretchy and will not pull and wrinkle the way fabric that is cut along the grain will. To cut bias strips, first cut a fabric square. Use a T-square to check that all corners of the square are precise 90-degree angles. Fold the square in half diagonally, and cut through both layers, as shown in **Figure F**. The distance between the fold line and the second cutting line determines the width of the bias strip.

Running stitches are the most basic stitches used for hand sewn seams. Pick up several small and evenly spaced stitches on your needle before pulling the thread through the fabric, as shown in **Figure G**.

Blind stitches are inconspicuous on both sides of the fabric. They are used for hemming, securing facings, or any place that hidden stitches are needed (**Figure H**).

Working with Pantyhose

The main thing to remember when soft-sculpting pantyhose is that you do not have to settle for what you get the first time. Stuffed hose are remarkably pliable and moldable – almost like working with clay. Even after a hose has been stuffed and tied off, you can manipulate the shape to an amazing degree. If you wish to enlarge a small area, you can use the tip of your needle to pull the fiberfill outward. For larger areas, you can manipulate the fiberfill using your hands. By working with the stuffed hose, you can arrange it to assume many characteristics.

It is easier to work with a shape that has not been overstuffed. You want just enough fiberfill to fill out the desired shape, but not so much that the hose is over-stretched and loses flexibility. If a shape is very tightly stuffed, there will be no room for the fiberfill to give when you wish to manipulate a specific shape.

Pantyhose seams can be machine stitched. Always stretch the hose gently as you sew. The stretching will space your stitches so they will not break when the hose is stretched along the seam. You can stretch the hose and stitch using a straight stitch or zig-zag stitch set on the narrowest width. Some sewing machines make stretch stitches.

When stuffing a head, use your fingers to mold the fiberfill into a head shape (not simply a round sphere). Remember not to stuff the head too tightly. Insert your hand inside the head to create a cavity in the core of the stuffing; you want to have plenty of give when you sculpt the facial features.

When attaching the head to the body, begin whipstitching at the center back, and continue around the neck. We've found that starting at any other point causes the head to swivel into a strange position.

A single length of heavy-duty thread about 18 to 20 inches long is usually sufficient to soft-sculpt all of the facial features. If this length proves to be too short, stop sculpting at a "lock the stitch" step, and cut the thread. Rethread your needle, enter at point 1 again, and continue sculpting at the next step.

In the instructions, "reenter at the same point" means that you should insert the needle as closely as possible to the last exit point. Do not try to find the precise exit point.

When the instructions tell you to pull the thread tightly, do so in a gentle manner, being careful not to rip the hose.

To secure the stitches temporarily as you are working on a section, take one or two tiny stitches under the surface. To lock the stitches permanently at the end of a section, take several small stitches at the designated point and knot the thread with each stitch.

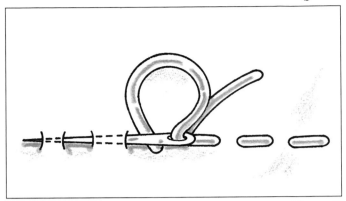

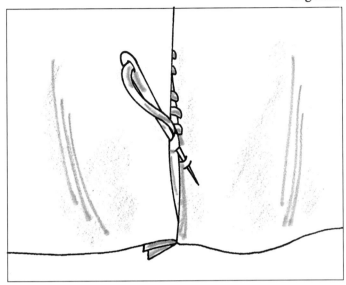

Figure H

If you see a run begin to develop, you can apply a small amount of clear nail polish to the end of the run, let the polish dry, and then continue working.

If you are just beginning, we suggest that you make a practice head before tackling a project. This will give you more confidence in working with soft-sculpted pantyhose.

When you have completed your pantyhose project, a light coating of spray-on clear acrylic will help protect the hose from dust, smudges, and runs.

Fabric Painting

Acrylic paint straight from the tube is usually a good thickness for fabric painting. If the paint begins to dry while you are working with it, add a drop of water and stir thoroughly. Paint that is too watery will bleed into the fabric; paint that is too thick will not penetrate the fibers. If you have never painted on fabric before, practice the technique on a scrap of the same material specified for the project.

One fine-point artist's brush is enough to begin fabric painting. You may want to add larger brushes later. Good brushes are expensive, but well worth the money. Never allow paint to dry in a brush. Acrylic paints are water soluble, but once dry, they are permanent.

Figure I

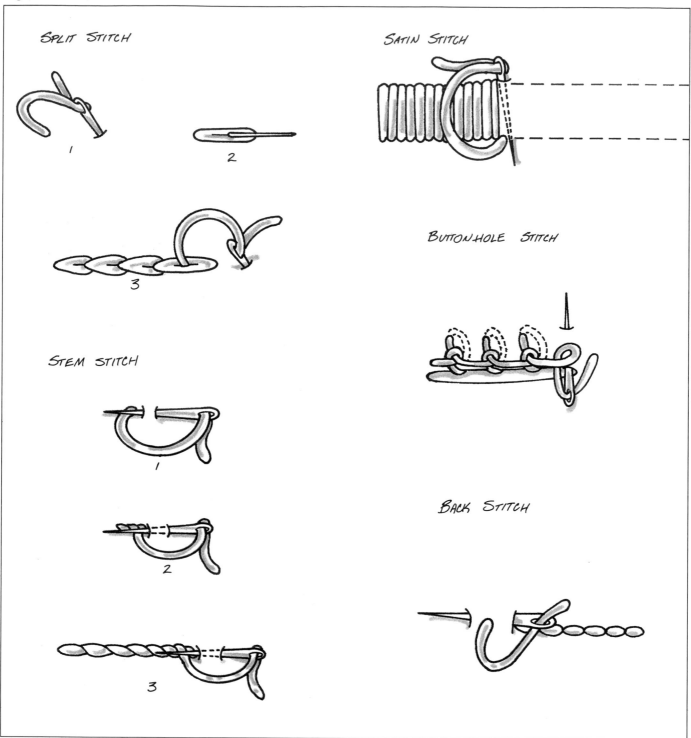

Embroidery

Cotton embroidery floss contains six strands that can be separated. The fewer strands you use, the smaller needle you need, the more stitches you will take, and the finer the finished work.

To avoid knotting the floss at the beginning of embroidery, work a running stitch on the surface, positioning it so that subsequent stitches will cover it. Finish a length of floss by running the end under the last few stitches on the wrong side of the work. Always use an embroidery hoop to hold your fabric while you work. We also suggest that you preshrink your fabric.

Illustrations of the embroidery stitches that you will use in the projects in this book are provided in **Figure G**. With a little practice, even a beginner can produce stitches that are smooth and even.

Materials

Gingham fabric: ¼ yard of pastel blue, ½ yard of pastel green, ¼ yard of pink, and ⅜ yard of yellow (Choose gingham fabrics with very tiny squares.)

⅝ yard of white muslin

⅝ yard of white eyelet fabric

3¾ yards of white eyelet trim, 1 inch wide

1¼ yards of white eyelet trim, 1½ inches wide

5 x 8-inch piece of pink double-knit (stretchy) fabric in a shade that coordinates with the pink gingham

4 x 4-inch piece of green felt

One leg cut from a pair of regular-weave, flesh-tone pantyhose, or one nylon stocking

Heavy-duty and regular white thread

Satin ribbon: 1 yard of pink and 2 yards of yellow, each ¼ inch wide; and 1 yard of yellow, 1 inch wide

Heavy cardboard: one 14 x 14-inch piece, and two 10 x 15-inch pieces, for backing

One small cardboard box, approximately 4 x 4 x 4 inches (It need not have a top.)

One bag of polyester fiberfill

Glue gun and hot-melt glue (If you prefer to use white glue, pin or tape all glued assemblies until they are dry.)

Two 18-inch lengths of ¼-inch-diameter wooden dowel rod

32-inch length of ¼ x 1¼-inch pine lattice or other similar wood (It need not be nicely finished wood, as it will be used across the back of the finished project to help secure the various parts together.)

Cosmetic cheek blusher

There are eleven parts to the wall hanging: three clouds, three rainbow stripes, one balloon, one gondola (balloon basket), and three babies. Each part is made separately, then all are joined in the final assembly.

Cutting the Pieces

1. Scale drawings for the Balloon, Large Cloud, and Small Cloud are provided in **Figure A**. Enlarge the drawings to make full-size patterns.

2. Full-size patterns for the Baby Body, Baby Cap, and Baby Cap Bill are provided in **Figure B**. Trace the patterns onto pattern or tracing paper, so you won't have to cut up your book.

3. Cut the pieces as listed here, from the specified fabrics.

Green gingham: Balloon – cut one
        Baby Body – cut two
Yellow gingham: Gondola – cut one, 5 x 5 inches
                      cut two, 5 x 18 inches
        Rainbow – cut one, 6 x 29 inches
Blue gingham: Rainbow – cut one, 6 x 29 inches
        Baby Body – cut two
Pink gingham: Rainbow – cut one, 6 x 29 inches
        Baby Body – cut two
White eyelet fabric: Large Cloud – cut two
              Small Cloud – cut two

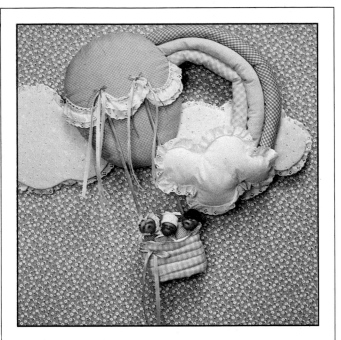

Baby Wall Hanging

Your little ones can float into dreamland in a gingham gondola with this easy-to-assemble wall hanging. Fluffy, white eyelet clouds play across the rainbow. The overall size is approximately 30 x 35 inches.

White muslin: Large Cloud – cut two
Green Felt: Baby Cap – cut one
          Baby Cap Bill – cut one
Cardboard: (Cut the Cardboard pieces one inch smaller
          than the pattern all the way around
          as indicated on the scale drawing.)
          Balloon – cut one from the 14 x 14-inch piece
          Large Cloud – cut one from each 10 x 15-inch piece

Making the Balloon

1. Glue a generous amount of fiberfill to one side of the cardboard Balloon piece. It should be an even depth all over, and should extend all the way to the edges.

2. Center the gingham Balloon piece right side up on top of the fiberfill and cardboard. Hold it in place as you turn the assembly upside down. Fold the edges of the gingham piece to the back of the cardboard and glue them in place all the way around. You need not stretch the fabric as you work, but be sure to pull it snugly. You want a smooth look on the front – but if you stretch the fabric, the nice, straight rows of gingham squares will be crooked.

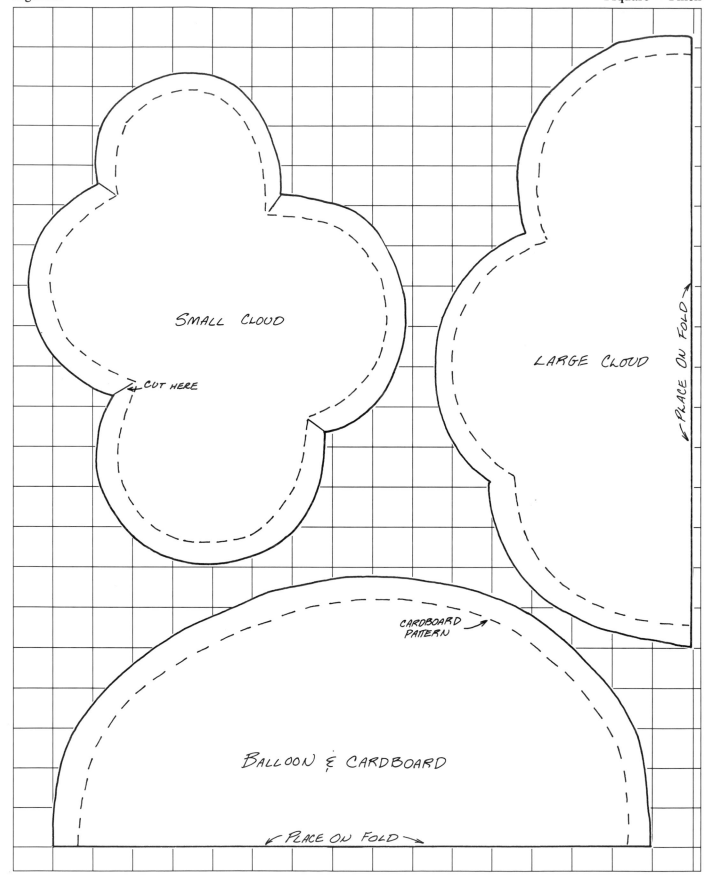

SMALL CLOUD

CUT HERE

LARGE CLOUD

PLACE ON FOLD

CARDBOARD
PATTERN

BALLOON & CARDBOARD

PLACE ON FOLD

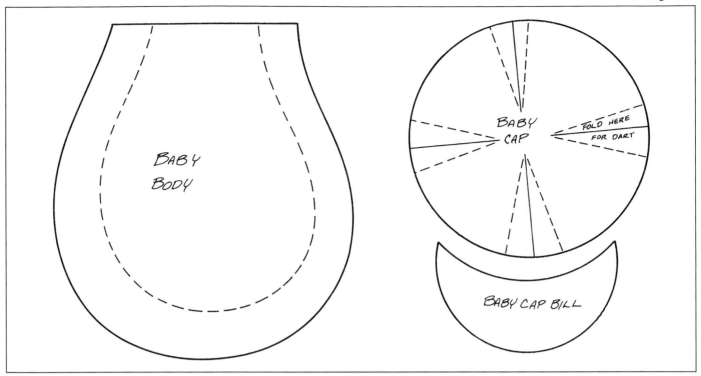

Figure C

Figure D

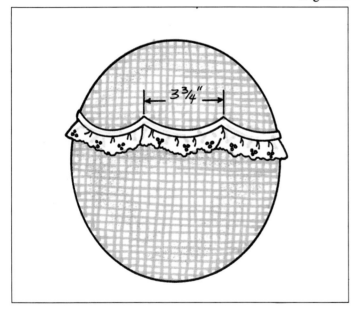

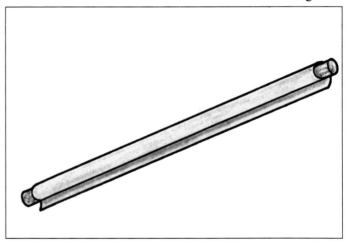

3. Cut the 1½-inch-wide white eyelet trim into two equal lengths. Pin one of the lengths to the front of the stuffed balloon, forming three large scallops, as shown in **Figure C**. Place this length of eyelet just above the horizontal center line of the balloon. (The balloon is taller than it is wide.) Leave plenty of eyelet at the points of the scallops, so it won't be pulled and stretched at these points. Fold the ends of the eyelet to the back of the cardboard, and glue or whipstitch the eyelet in place. Attach the remaining length of eyelet to the balloon in the same manner, just above and overlapping the first length.

4. Cut the 1-inch-wide yellow ribbon into two equal lengths. Wrap and glue one length around each of the dowel rods, as shown in **Figure D**. Glue the covered dowel rods to the front of the balloon, inserting the ends up under the eyelet trim at the points of the scallops, as shown in **Figure E**. Each rod should be turned so that the lapped edge of the ribbon covering faces the balloon.

5. Cut two 1-yard lengths of narrow pink ribbon, and two 1-yard lengths of narrow yellow ribbon. Place one yellow and one pink length together, and tie a small bow at the center. Tack or glue the bow to the front of the balloon, just above the point of one scallop. Cut the ends of the ribbons at an angle, and allow them to hang free. Repeat these procedures, using the remaining two lengths of ribbon, and attach them just above the point of the remaining scallop on the front of the balloon.

Figure E

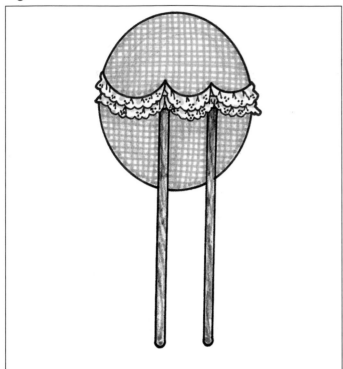

Figure F

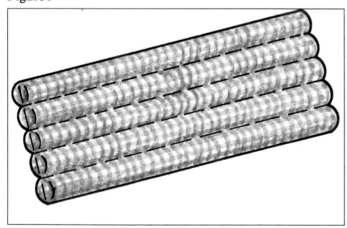

Figure G

Figure H

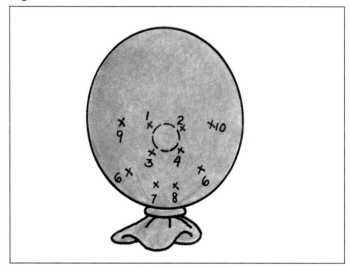

Making the Gondola

1. Glue the smaller yellow Gondola piece to the bottom of the small cardboard box, wrapping all four edges up onto the sides and glueing them in place.

2. The two larger yellow Gondola pieces will be stitched together and stuffed to cover the sides of the gondola box. Place the two pieces right sides together and stitch a ½-inch-wide seam along both long edges and one short edge. Leave the remaining short edge open and unstitched. Clip the corners, turn the assembly right side out, and press. Press the seam allowances to the inside along the open raw edges. Stuff it lightly and evenly with fiberfill, and whipstitch the opening edges together.

3. To give the gondola a soft, puffy look, run four evenly spaced lines of topstitching through all thicknesses along the length of the stuffed assembly (**Figure F**).

4. Wrap and glue the stuffed cover around the gondola box. Whipstitch the ends together at the back.

5. Cut a 17-inch length of eyelet trim and glue it to the upper edge of the gondola box, on the inside. The scalloped edge of the eyelet should extend up above the box. Overlap the ends of the eyelet at the back of the box.

6. Cut a 1-yard length of narrow pink ribbon. Tie a small bow at the center, cut the ends at an angle, and tack or glue the bow to the front center of the gondola box. Allow the ends of the ribbon to hang free.

Making the Babies

We made three babies for the wall hanging. Each is assembled in the same manner, except for the caps.

1. To make one head, cut a 5-inch length from the pantyhose leg or stocking. You should now have a 5-inch-long nylon tube. Slit the tube so you have a flat rectangle of nylon. Wrap it around a small ball of fiberfill, gather the hose around the fiberfill, and twist the hose beneath the fiberfill (**Figure G**). The head should be about 2½ inches in diameter from top to bottom,

Figure I

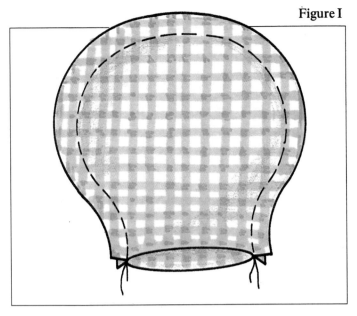

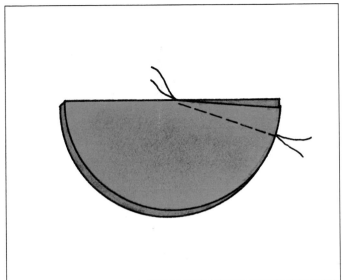

and 7½ inches in circumference around the eye line. Add or remove fiberfill until the head is the correct size, then wrap the twisted hose tightly with heavy-duty thread. Cut off most of the excess hose below the thread.

2. Use a sharp needle and a length of heavy-duty thread to sculpt the facial features, following the entry and exit points illustrated in **Figure H**.

a. Enter where the hose is tied at the neck, pass through the center of the head, and exit at point 1. Sew a clockwise circle of deep basting stitches about ½ inch in diameter (passing through points 2, 4, 3, and 1 again), and exit at point 2.

b. Use the tip of the needle to carefully lift fiberfill within the circle, just enough to make a small bulge. Gently pull the thread until a little round nose appears inside the circle.

c. Lock the stitch, exiting at 1.

d. To form the nostrils, reenter at 1 and exit at point 3. Reenter just barely above 3, on the nose, and exit at 2.

e. Pull the thread gently and maintain the tension as you reenter at 2 and exit at 4. Reenter just barely above 4, on the nose, and exit at 1.

f. Pull the thread gently and maintain the tension as you take another tiny stitch at point 1 to lock the stitches.

g. Continue working with the same length of thread to form the mouth. Reenter at 1 and exit at 5. Pull the thread across the surface, enter at 6, and exit at 1. Pull the thread until a smile appears, and lock the stitch.

h. To form the bottom lip, reenter at 1 and exit at 2. Reenter at 2 and exit at 7. Pull the thread across the surface, enter at 8, and exit at 2. Pull the thread gently until the lower lip appears, and lock the stitch.

i. To form the eyes, reenter at 2 and exit at 9. Pull the thread across the surface, enter at 1, and exit at 10. Pull the thread across the surface, enter at 2, and exit at 1. Gently pull the thread until tiny, closed eyes appear. Lock the stitch.

j. Reenter at 1, guide the needle through the head to the neck, and exit at your original entry point. Pull the thread taut, lock the stitch, and cut the thread.

3. Brush cosmetic blusher over the cheeks.

4. Repeat the procedures in steps 1, 2, and 3 to make two more baby heads, or as many as you like.

5. Place the two green gingham Body pieces right sides together and stitch the seam along the long curved edge, leaving the short, straight upper edge open and unstitched (**Figure I**). Clip the curve, turn the body right side out, and press. Press the seam allowances to the inside along the open raw edges.

6. Stuff the body with fiberfill. Run a line of basting stitches around the open neck edge, but do not cut off the tails of thread, so you can gather the neck opening.

7. Place a head on top of the body, inserting the excess hose below the neck into the neck opening of the body. Pull the threads to gather the neck edge of the body, and securely whipstitch the body to the head around the neck.

8. Repeat the procedures in steps 5 and 6 to create two more baby bodies, using the remaining blue and pink Body pieces. Attach a head to each body as described in step 7.

Making the Baby Caps

1. For one baby, cut a 6-inch length of eyelet trim and wrap it around the head in bonnet fashion. Glue or whipstitch it in place, hiding the ends at the back.

2. The second cap is a baseball-style cap. Stitch four tiny darts in the Baby Cap piece. To make a dart, fold the Cap piece along one of the fold lines indicated on the pattern. Run an angled line of stitches as indicated on the pattern, from the outer edge up to the fold. Tie off the threads at both ends of the dart, as shown in **Figure J**. Stitch three more darts in the same manner, referring to the pattern for placement. Fold the fabric the same way each time, so all the darts are on the same side of the fabric. Press all the darts flat.

3. Turn the cap right side out, so the darts are on the inside. Glue or whipstitch the Bill piece to the cap, and glue or whipstitch the assembled cap to one of the baby's heads.

Figure K

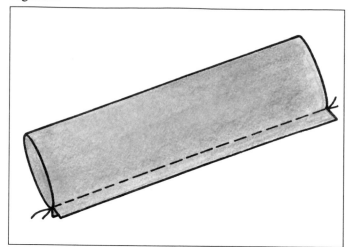

Figure L

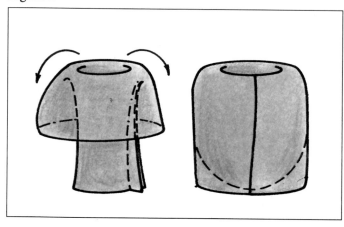

Figure M

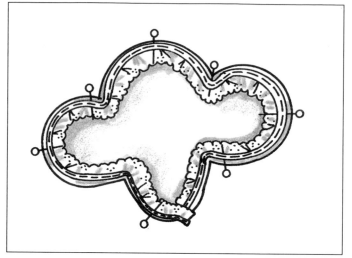

4. Use the piece of pink, stretchy fabric for the third cap. Fold the fabric in half lengthwise, placing right sides together, and stitch a narrow seam along the long edge only (**Figure K**). Leave both short ends open and unstitched. You should now have a tube.

5. Fold the stitched tube in half, pulling one end down toward the other so you have a double thickness with the seam allowances on the inside and the raw edges together (**Figure L**).

6. Position the vertical seam in the center and stitch a curved seam through all four layers, close to the raw edges, as shown in **Figure L**. Trim the seam allowance evenly to about ¼ inch, and turn the cap right side out. Place it over the remaining baby's head. Cut a 6- or 8-inch length of narrow pink ribbon, tie it in a bow, and glue or whipstitch the bow to the cap.

7. Use any remaining lengths of excess ribbon to tie bows around the babies' necks.

Finishing the Gondola

1. Fill the bottom of the gondola with fiberfill.

2. The gondola is attached to the dowels that you previously glued to the balloon. Insert the free lower end of each dowel into the gondola, and glue them to the inside of the back wall.

3. Place the three babies in the gondola, adjusting the amount of fiberfill in the bottom of the box as needed. The babies may be glued in place or left unattached.

Making the Large Clouds

1. Place one muslin Large Cloud piece against the wrong side of one eyelet Large Cloud piece and baste around the edges. This will hold the pieces together for step 2.

2. Center the lined Large Cloud piece over one of the cardboard Large Cloud pieces. Clip the fabric at each corner (as indicated on the scale drawing) up to each corner of the cardboard piece. Turn the entire assembly face down and glue the edges of the fabric to the back of the cardboard, keeping the fabric smooth on the front as you work.

3. Cut a 38-inch length of eyelet trim. Glue the bound edge of the trim to the back of the cardboard, close to the edge all the way around. The scalloped edge of the eyelet should extend beyond the edge of the cloud. Overlap the ends of the eyelet and glue them neatly to the back of the cardboard.

4. Repeat the procedures in steps 1, 2, and 3 to create a second large cloud, using the remaining cardboard, muslin, and eyelet-fabric Large Cloud pieces.

Making the Small Cloud

1. Place one of the Small Cloud pieces right side up on a flat surface. Cut a 34-inch length of eyelet trim. Pin the bound edge of the trim along the edge of the Small Cloud piece, so that the scalloped edge of the trim extends in toward the center of the fabric piece (**Figure M**). Be sure to allow plenty of trim at each corner, so it won't be stretched flat when it is turned outward later. Overlap the ends of the trim, allowing them to extend out beyond the edge of the fabric piece. Baste the trim in place.

2. Place the remaining Small Cloud piece right side down on top of the first one. The eyelet will be sandwiched between the two fabric pieces. Stitch the seam around the entire edge of the cloud, leaving a 3-inch opening between the beginning and end of the seam. Clip the seam allowances at each corner and at intervals along each curve.

3. Turn the cloud right side out and press gently. Press the seam allowances to the inside along the edges of the opening. The eyelet should now extend outward around the edge of the cloud. Stuff the cloud with fiberfill, and whipstitch the opening edges together.

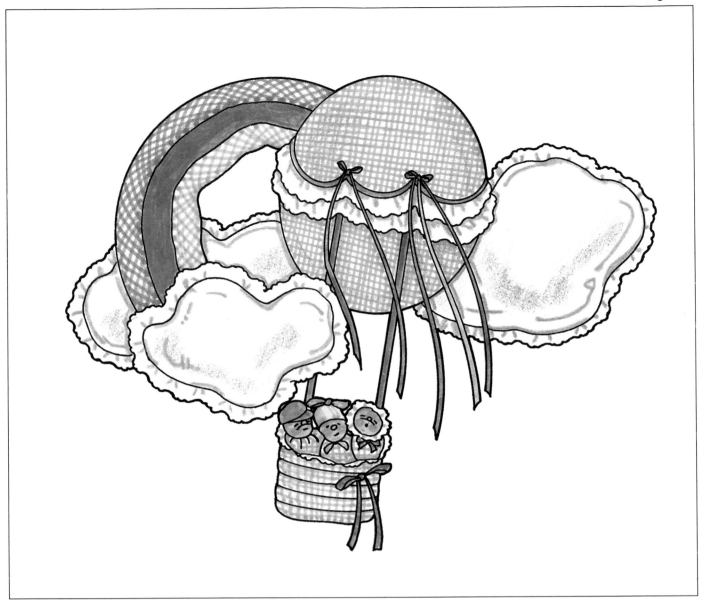

Making the Rainbow

1. Fold one of the Rainbow pieces in half lengthwise, placing right sides together, and stitch a ½-inch-wide seam along the long edge and one short end. Leave the remaining short end open and unstitched. Clip the corners.

2. Turn the stitched rectangle right side out and stuff it with fiberfill. Turn the seam allowances to the inside at the open end and whipstitch the end closed.

3. Repeat the procedures in steps 1 and 2 to stitch, turn, and stuff each of the remaining two Rainbow pieces. These three tubes will be the rainbow stripes.

Final Assembly

1. An outline drawing of the assembled wall hanging is provided in **Figure N**. Work on a large flat surface. Begin by placing the two large clouds right sides up in the positions shown.

Place the balloon/gondola assembly on top, so that the balloon overlaps each of the large clouds as shown. Glue the balloon to both clouds.

2. Now add the rainbow stripes, beginning with the top one. Glue one end of the tube to the back of the balloon where indicated in **Figure N**. (Be sure that the seam in the rainbow stripe is facing the back.) Curl the tube downward and glue the free end to the front of the large cloud as shown. Add the remaining two rainbow stripes in the same manner. They can be glued to one another if they tend to separate, but this should not be a problem.

3. Glue the stuffed small cloud over the lower ends of the rainbow stripes, and to the left-hand dowel rod of the balloon.

4. Allow enough time for the glue to set up, and then carefully turn the entire assembly face down. Glue the strip of lattice or other wood across the backs of the large clouds and the balloon, to strengthen the assembly.

Clown Music Box

Pretty to look at and lovely to hear, this music box will delight both the young and the young-at-heart. Select the musical movement of your choice and let the Pierrot-style clown dance to the tune. Overall height is about 14 inches.

Materials

For the Clown:

¼ yard of white satin-finish polyester fabric
Small scrap of black satin-finish polyester fabric
1 yard of black bias tape
4 x 6-inch piece of black felt
Small amount of polyester fiberfill
Two black ½-inch-diameter buttons
Three fancy black buttons for the hat
Several chenille pipe cleaners, one of which must be black
One leg cut from a pair of nurse's white pantyhose, or one white nylon stocking
Heavy-duty white thread and a long sharp needle
Black fine felt-tip marker
Fabric glue or hot-melt glue and a glue gun

For the Base:

8 x 10-inch piece of ¾-inch-thick oak or veneer-core plywood with a nice finish
5 x 6-inch piece of ¼-inch-thick oak or veneer-core plywood

1-inch length of 1½-inch-diameter wooden closet rod
2-inch length of ⅜-inch-diameter wooden dowel rod
8-inch length of ³⁄₁₆-inch-diameter wooden dowel rod
A few thin wood scraps
Standard wind-up musical movement
Wire brads, carpenter's wood glue, and wood stain

Cutting the Pieces

1. Scale drawings for the Sleeve, Blouse, Pants, Cap, and Hat are provided in **Figure A**. Enlarge the drawings to make full-size patterns.

2. Full-size patterns for the Slipper and Leg are provided in **Figure B**. Trace the patterns onto dressmaker's pattern paper or tracing paper.

3. Cut the pieces for the clown as listed below, from the specified fabrics.

White pantyhose: Head – cut one 6-inch-diameter circle
                Hands – cut two 2-inch-diameter circles
White polyester: Hat – cut one
             Collar – cut two 6-inch-diameter circles
             Blouse – cut two
             Sleeve – cut four
             Pants – cut two
             Leg – cut two
Black polyester: Cap – cut two
Black felt: Umbrella – cut one 2-inch-diameter circle
        Slipper – cut four

4. Cut the pieces for the base as listed below, from ¾-inch oak or plywood.

Description	Quantity	Dimension in inches
Front/Back	2	3 x 5¼
Side	2	3 x 3

5. Cut one base top, 4½ x 5¼ inches, from ¼-inch solid oak or plywood.

THE CLOWN
Making the Head

1. Wrap the 6-inch-diameter circle of white pantyhose around a 4-inch-diameter ball of polyester fiberfill. Gather the raw edge of the hose and tie it off using thread. This will be the bottom of the head.

2. Manipulate the shape until a head is formed (**Figure C**). It should be about 1½ inches in diameter across the eyeline, and longer than it is wide.

3. Use a long sharp needle and heavy-duty thread to sculpt the facial features. Follow the entry and exit points illustrated in **Figure D**.

   a. Enter at 1 (where the hose is tied at the neck) and exit at 2. To form the nose, sew a circle of basting stitches approximately ½ inch in diameter, exiting at 3.

1 square = 1 inch

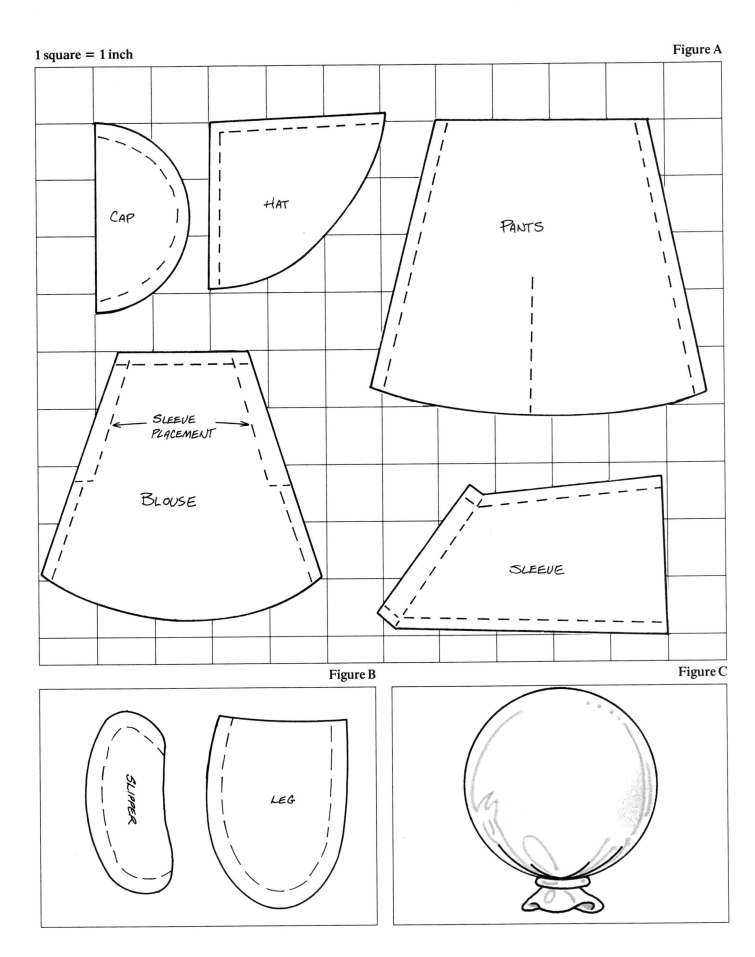

CAP

HAT

PANTS

SLEEVE
PLACEMENT

BLOUSE

SLEEVE

Figure B

Figure C

SLIPPER

LEG

CLOWN MUSIC BOX

Figure D

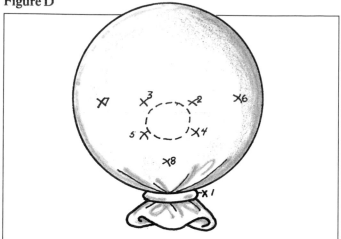

Figure E

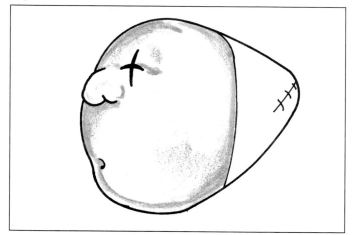

Figure F

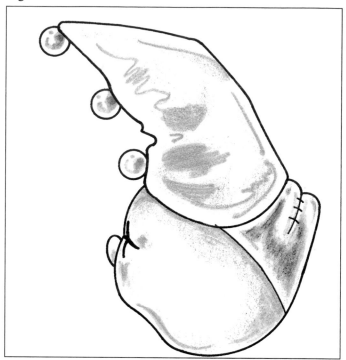

Figure G

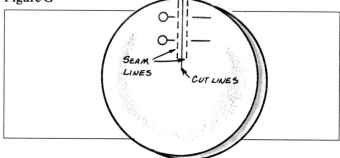

b. Use the tip of the needle to carefully lift the fiberfill within the circle, just enough to make a small bulge. Gently pull the thread until a nice round nose appears.

c. Lock the stitch under the bridge of the nose, exiting at point 2.

d. To form the nostrils, reenter at 2 and exit at 4.

e. Reenter ¼ inch above 4 on the nose, and exit at 3.

f. Reenter at 3 and exit at 5.

g. Reenter ¼ inch above 5 and exit at 2. Lock the stitch under the bridge of the nose and exit at 2.

4. To form the eyes and mouth, continue with the same thread and again follow the entry and exit points shown in **Figure D**.

    a. Reenter at 2 and exit at 6.

    b. Pull the thread across the surface, enter at 2, and exit at point 3.

    c. Reenter at 3 and exit at 7.

    d. Pull the thread across the surface, enter at 3, and exit at 2. Gently pull the thread until the closed eyes appear. Lock the stitch.

    e. Reenter at 2 and exit at 1. Lock the stitch at 1 and cut the thread.

    f. To form the mouth, enter at 8 and exit at 1.

    g. Gently pull the thread until a little O-shaped mouth appears, then lock the stitch and cut the thread.

5. Draw a line over each eye stitch, using a black felt-tip marker. Draw a vertical line of about the same length across each eye line. Color the mouth as well.

Making the Hat and Collar

1. Place the two Cap pieces right sides together and stitch the seam along the long curved edge. Clip the curve and turn the cap right side out. Glue it to the back of the clown head, turning the raw edge under as you glue (**Figure E**).

2. Fold the Hat piece in half, placing right sides together, and stitch the seam along the straight edges. Press the seam open. Turn a ¼-inch hem to the wrong side of the fabric along the long curved edge, and stitch. Turn the hat right side out to form a cone. Glue three fancy black buttons to the front of the hat, and then glue the hat to the clown head, placing the seam at the back, as shown in **Figure F**.

3. To make the collar, place the two circular Collar pieces right sides together, and cut along the radius of the circles, as shown in **Figure G**. Pin the two circles together along the cut. Stitch each seam, leaving ¼ inch unstitched at the center of the circle for the neck opening. Press each seam open, and open out the two circles.

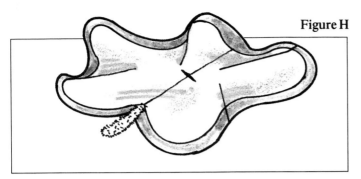
Figure H

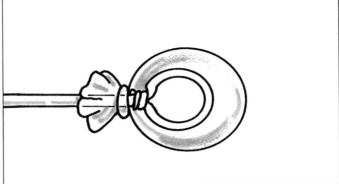
Figure J

Figure I

Figure K
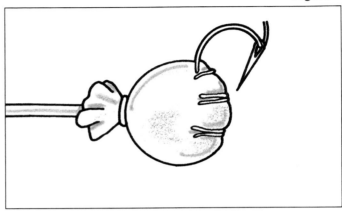

3. To sculpt the fingers, take three evenly spaced stitches through the hand, wrapping the thread around the end of the hand, as shown in **Figure K**. Pull the thread to form little fingers. Return the thread to the wrist and lock the stitch.

4. Repeat steps 2 and 3 at the opposite end of the pipe cleaner to form the second hand.

Making the Arms and Body

1. Place the two Blouse pieces right sides together and stitch the shoulder seam along the short straight edge, leaving a ¼-inch neck opening at the center. Press the seam open.

2. Place two Sleeve pieces right sides together and stitch the seam along the longest edge. Press the sleeve open.

3. Place the blouse on a flat surface, right side up. Pin the upper edge of the sleeve to the blouse, placing right sides together, and aligning the sleeve seam with the shoulder seam (**Figure L**). Stitch the seam and press the seam allowances toward the blouse.

4. Follow the procedures described in steps 2 and 3 to assemble a second sleeve. Stitch it to the opposite side edge of the blouse in the same manner.

5. Fold the blouse in half, right sides together, and stitch the underarm and side seam on each side, as shown in **Figure M**. Press the seams open.

6. Turn the blouse right side out and hem the lower edge. Hem the lower edge of each sleeve.

7. Stitch or glue two black buttons to the center front line of the blouse.

4. Encase the entire outer edge of the collar, using black bias tape, but do not stitch the ends closed, because the tape will form a casing for a pipe cleaner. Twist together two pipe cleaners end to end, and thread them through the casing (**Figure H**), so you can form permanent ruffles later. Gather the neck opening of the collar using a needle and heavy thread.

5. Place the head in the center of the collar, on the right side of the fabric. Pull the excess hose through the neck opening of the collar, to the wrong side, and whipstitch around the neck to secure the head to the collar. To form the large ruffles, bend the outer edge of the collar, as shown in **Figure I**.

Making the Hands

1. Form a ½-inch-diameter loop at each end of a pipe cleaner. A hand will be attached to each end.

2. To make one hand, form a small ball of fiberfill around the loop at one end of the pipe cleaner, and wrap it with the 2-inch-diameter circle of white pantyhose (**Figure J**). Gather the raw edge of the hose at the wrist and tie it off, using thread.

Figure L

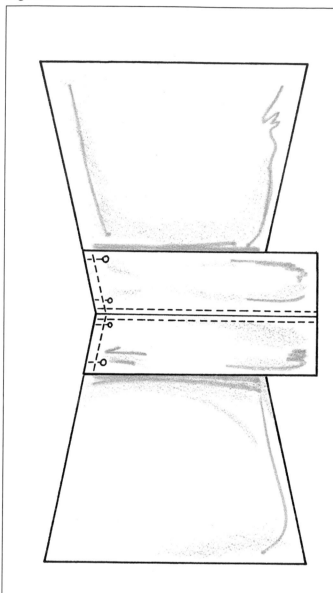

Figure M

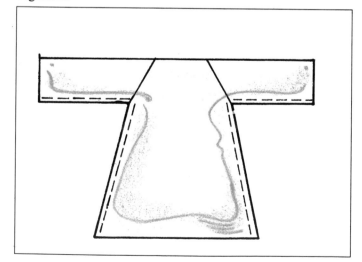

Figure N

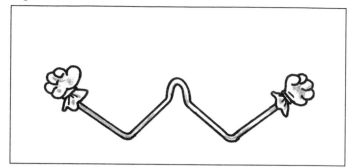

Figure O

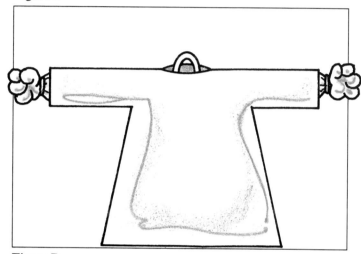

Figure P

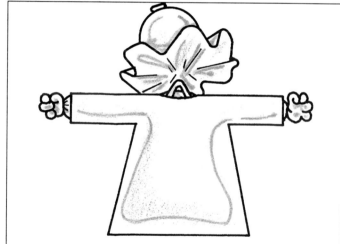

Assembling the Torso

1. Bend the pipe cleaner with the hands on it into a "W" shape (**Figure N**). Insert the pipe cleaner into the blouse, and push one hand out the end of each sleeve (**Figure O**).

2. The center of the "W" will serve as the neck. Insert it up into the head from beneath the collar and glue it securely in place (**Figure P**).

3. Gather the lower edge of each sleeve around the wrist, using heavy thread.

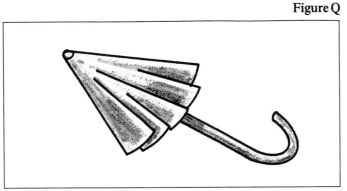

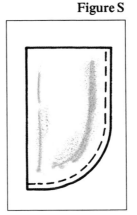

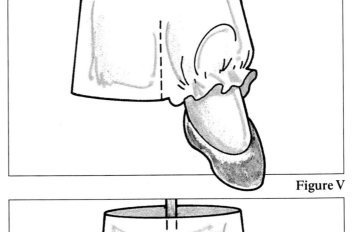

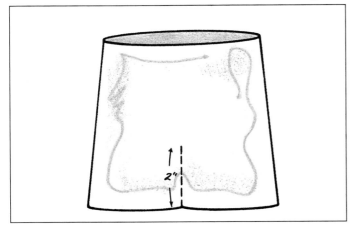

Figure V

4. Lightly stuff each sleeve with polyester fiberfill. Stuff the shoulder and chest area of the blouse as well.

5. To make the umbrella, cut a small slit at the center of the black felt Umbrella piece, and slip one end of the black pipe cleaner through it. Cut a 1½-inch length from the opposite end of the pipe cleaner. Gather the slit around the pipe cleaner, as shown in **Figure Q**. Use the cut length of the pipe cleaner to secure the gathered edge. Bend a hook at the handle end of the umbrella and hang it on one of the clown's hands.

Making the Pants, Legs, and Slippers

1. Place the two Pants pieces right sides together and stitch the side seams, leaving the upper and lower edges open. Press the seams open. Hem the lower edge of the pants.

2. Turn the pants right side out and topstitch through both layers along the vertical center line, from the lower edge upward (**Figure R**).

3. To make one leg, fold one Leg piece in half lengthwise and stitch the seam along the curved edge. Leave the straight upper edge open (**Figure S**). Clip the curve and turn the leg right side out. Lightly stuff the leg with fiberfill.

4. Make another leg in the same manner.

5. To make one slipper, place two Slipper pieces right sides together and stitch the seam along the long curved edges. Leave the upper edge unstitched. Clip the curve and turn the slipper right side out.

6. Make another slipper in the same manner.

7. Place one slipper over each foot (the curved end of each leg), and glue it in place (**Figure T**).

8. Insert the upper end of a leg into one of the openings at the lower edge of the pants, leaving the foot extending about 1 inch from the pants (**Figure U**). Gather the pants around the leg, and whipstitch the leg to the gathered pants, using heavy-duty thread.

9. Stitch the remaining leg to the pants in the same manner, but insert the 8-inch-length of ³⁄₁₆-inch wooden dowel rod into the pants opening before you stitch it closed (**Figure V**). The clown assembly will be completed after you have made the wooden base.

Figure W

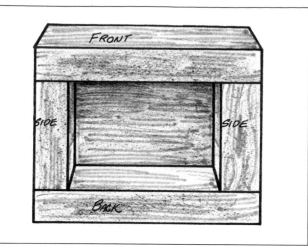

Figure X

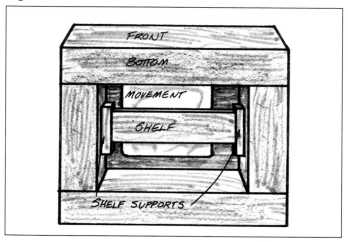

Figure Y

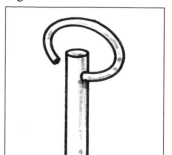

Figure Z

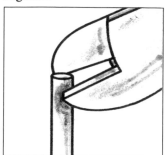

Figure AA

THE BASE

1. Assemble a rectangular box using the Front, Back, and Side pieces, butting the edges, as shown in **Figure W**. Glue all of the joints.

2. Drill a hole through the center of the Top piece, large enough to accommodate the shaft of the musical movement you purchased. Glue the top to the box.

3. Stain the box and the 1-inch length of closet rod.

4. Insert the shaft of the musical movement from inside the box through the hole in the Top. Secure the movement by building a small shelf from thin wood scraps, as shown in **Figure X**. Attach the shelf and supports to the box sides, using glue and wire brads.

5. Remove the ring from the winding shaft of the musical movement (**Figure Y**), and discard it. The upper end of this shaft will be inserted into the clown's pedestal. So the pedestal will not slip on the shaft when it turns, make a burr on each side of the shaft, using a pair of diagonal wire cutters. Insert the tip of one cutter blade into the small hole in the shaft that held the ring (**Figure Z**). Squeeze the cutters to make a burr. Do the same on the other side of the shaft.

6. The 1-inch-length of 1½-inch-diameter closet rod will serve as the pedestal. Drill a socket the same diameter as the

musical movement shaft, into the center of the pedestal on one side. To determine the depth of the socket, measure the length of the shaft extending above the base. Drill the socket the same length. Unscrew the shaft from the musical movement and press the burred end of the shaft into the socket in the pedestal. When the shaft is screwed back onto the movement, the bottom of the pedestal will be nearly flush with the top of the box.

7. Drill a ³⁄₁₆-inch-diameter socket, ½ inch deep, into the opposite side of the pedestal, ¼ inch from the edge. Insert the lower end of the dowel rod with the clown's legs on it into the socket, and glue it in place (**Figure AA**). Glue the clown's heels to the edge of the pedestal.

8. To elevate the box and allow the sound of the musical movement to be heard, cut four short legs from ⅜-inch-diameter dowel rod. Each should be about ⅜ inch long. Glue them to the bottom of the box, one at each corner, and secure each leg, using wire brads.

Final Assembly

1. Insert the shaft back through the base top and screw it into the musical movement.

2. Lightly stuff the clown's pants with fiberfill, and spot glue the fiberfill and pants to the dowel rod so they will stay in place.

3. Glue some fiberfill around the portion of the dowel rod that extends above the clown's pants. Shape the fiberfill into a cone with the small end on top (**Figure BB**).

4. Install the clown's upper body on the dowel rod. He should stand up fairly straight, so it may be necessary to spot glue inside the blouse (**Figure CC**).

CLOWN MUSIC BOX

Aunt Goldie

She's a life-size "livin' doll," ready to greet your guests, amaze the children, and offer quiet comfort to troubled minds. You can whisper your secrets into her understanding ear...she won't gossip! Aunt Goldie is also ready to house-sit for you. Simply sit her in a chair by a window and passers-by will think there is someone at home.

Materials

One regular-weave flesh-tone stocking or one leg from a pair of pantyhose, for the head
One pair of knee-high hose for the hands
3 yards of muslin for the body
¾ yard of calico fabric for the bonnet
Five bags of polyester fiberfill (If you want Aunt Goldie to be plump, you may need six bags.)
5-inch length of ¼-inch-wide elastic
Acrylic paints in white, blue, and black; and an artist's fine-tipped paint brush
A long sharp needle; regular thread to match the calico; and heavy-duty flesh-tone thread
Cosmetic cheek blusher
1-yard length of string

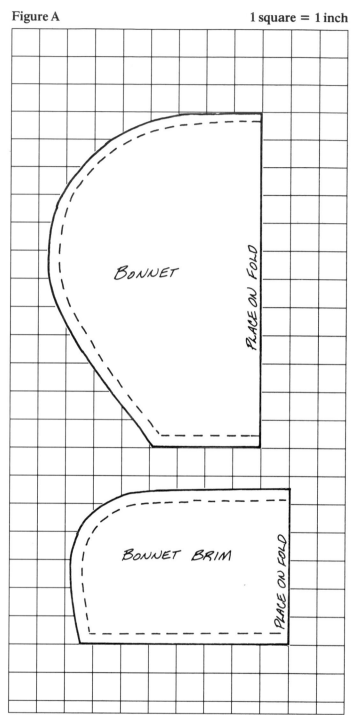

Figure A   1 square = 1 inch

Clothing

Note: You can dress Aunt Goldie in outgrown clothing and shoes, or you can purchase them for next to nothing at a local thrift shop.
A dress or a skirt and blouse (The size of the clothing will determine the size of Aunt Goldie. We used a full-length cream-colored dress with eyelet trim and a belt.)
One pair of ladies' boots (We used leather granny boots.)
A shawl to coordinate with the dress
A wig (We used a gray wig.)

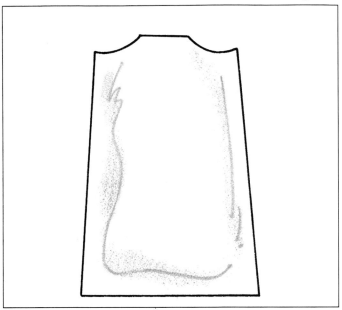

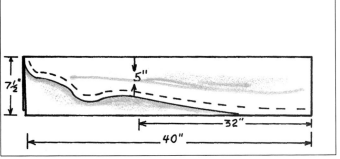

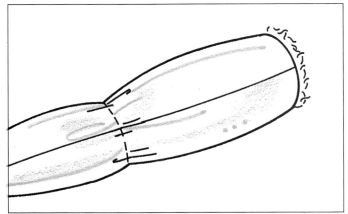

Figure C

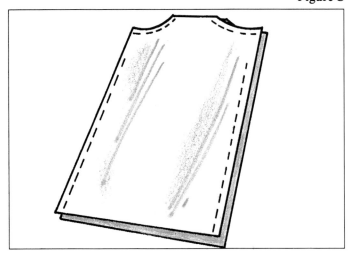

Cutting the Pieces

1. Scale drawings for the Bonnet and Bonnet Brim are provided in **Figure A**. Enlarge the drawings to make full-size patterns. Cut one Bonnet and two Bonnet Brims from calico. In addition, cut two Bonnet Ties, each 5 x 18 inches from calico.

2. The torso consists of two rectangular muslin pieces. To determine the size of each Torso piece, first measure around the waist of the dress Aunt Goldie will be wearing. The width of each Torso piece should be one-half the size of the waist, plus 1 inch. To determine the length of each Torso piece, measure the dress from the top of one shoulder to the waist and add 7 inches. Cut two muslin Torso pieces, including the neck. The Torso pieces should be shaped, as shown in **Figure B**.

3. To determine the length of each Arm piece, measure one of the dress sleeves from shoulder to wrist. Cut two muslin Arm pieces, each 11 inches wide and 1 inch longer than the sleeve measurement of the dress.

4. Cut two muslin Legs, each 15 x 40 inches.

Making the Body Parts

Note: All seams are ½ inch wide unless otherwise specified in the instructions.

1. Place the Torso pieces together and stitch the seams, as shown in **Figure C**, leaving the neck and lower edges open. Leave arm openings as shown.

2. To make one arm, fold one Arm piece in half lengthwise and stitch a seam along the long edge and one short edge, leaving the remaining short edge open. Clip the corners, turn the arm right side out, and stuff with fiberfill.

3. Make a second arm in the same manner. The hands will be added later.

4. To begin making one leg, fold one Leg piece in half lengthwise. Stitch a contoured seam, as shown in **Figure D**. The open end will be the top of the leg, and the contoured end will be the foot. The seam will run along the center back of the leg and the bottom of the foot. Trim the seam allowance to ½ inch along the contoured seam. Clip the curves and corners, turn the leg right side out, and stuff with fiberfill. (**Note:** If you want the legs to be shorter, cut a portion from the top of the leg.)

5. To make the knee bendable, measure approximately 18 inches from the upper end of the leg, and mark the leg using a pin or marker. Machine stitch across the width of the leg through all layers, as shown in **Figure E**.

6. Repeat steps 4 and 5 to make a second leg.

Assembling the Body

1. The torso should still be wrong side out. Insert one arm inside the torso and pin the open shoulder edge of the arm to

Figure F

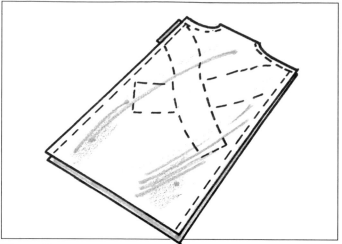

Figure G

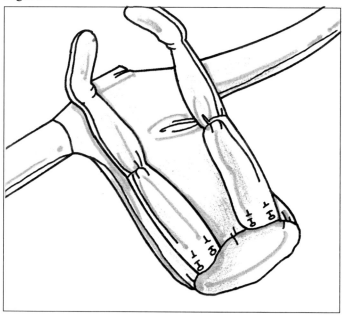

Figure H

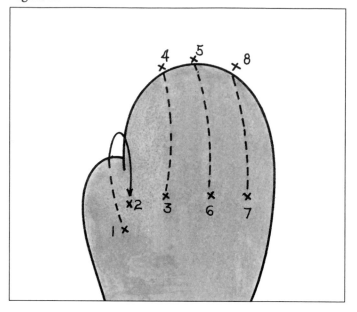

one armhole edge of the torso, as shown in **Figure F**. Pin the second arm in place in the same manner as you did the first. Stitch the two Torso pieces together along each armhole, with the arms sandwiched between.

2. Turn the torso right side out and stuff with fiberfill, leaving ½ inch unstuffed at the neck.

3. Pin the tops of the legs to the lower edge of the front torso, with the toes pointing toward the body (**Figure G**). Stitch ¼ inch from the edge to attach the legs to the front torso only.

4. Turn the legs downward and turn a ¼-inch seam allowance to the inside around the remaining portion of the lower edge. Whipstitch the pressed front and back lower edges together.

Making the Hands

1. To make one hand, stuff the foot portion of one knee-high stocking until it is approximately 8 inches in diameter. Make a second hand in the same manner. Keep them as equal in size as possible.

2. To soft-sculpt the fingers, follow the entry and exit points illustrated in **Figure H**, using a long sharp needle and heavy-duty thread.

    a. Flatten the hand, and insert the needle on the back of the hand, 5 inches from the wrist end, at point 1. Push the needle straight through the hand and exit on the palm side. This will be the base of the thumb.

    b. Pinch up a ridge on the thumb side of the hand. Wrap the thread around what will be the end of the thumb, enter at 2 on the back, and exit at 1 on the palm side.

    c. Pull the thread and lock the stitch. Reenter at 1 and exit at 3.

    d. Stitch up and down through the hand along the dotted line between 3 and 4.

    e. Enter at 4 and exit at 5. Gently pull the thread and lock the stitch.

    f. To form the last three fingers, repeat the procedures in steps d and e, stitching between 5 and 6 and then between 7 and 8.

    g. Lock the last stitch and cut the thread.

3. Wrap the thread loosely around the outside of the wrist. Lock the stitch and cut the thread.

4. Repeat the procedures in steps 2 and 3 to soft-sculpt the fingers on the remaining hand.

5. Slip the open wrist edge of one hand over the lower end of one arm. Trim the excess hose and whipstitch the hand in place. Attach the remaining hand in the same manner.

Making the Head

1. To form the head, tie a knot at the panty line of one leg of regular pantyhose. Cut 1 inch above the knot. Cut again 14 inches below the knot. Turn the hose so the knot is on the inside.

2. Stuff generous amounts of fiberfill inside the hose, manipulating the shape until a head is formed (**Figure I**). The completed head should be approximately the size of your own. Tie the hose loosely at the neck, using string.

Figure I

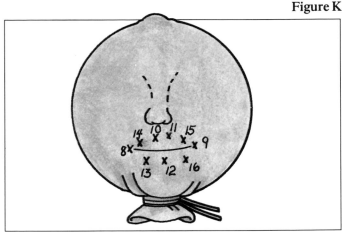

Figure K

Figure J

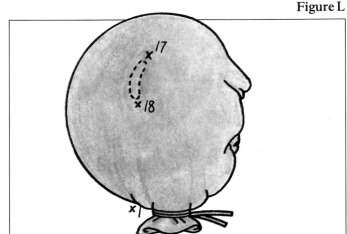

Figure L

3. To soft-sculpt the facial features, follow the entry and exit points illustrated in **Figure J**.

   a. Enter at 1 where the hose is tied at the neck, and exit at 2. Pinch up a vertical ridge approximately 1 inch wide in the center of the face. Stitch back and forth under the ridge, exiting at 3.

   b. Use the tip of the needle to carefully lift the fiberfill along the ridge. Pull the thread and lock the stitch at 3.

   c. To form the nostrils, reenter at 3 and exit at 4.

   d. Reenter ¼ inch above 4 and exit at 3.

   e. Reenter at 3 and exit at 5.

   f. Reenter at 5 and exit at 6.

   g. Reenter ¼ inch above 6 and exit at 7. Pull the thread and lock the stitch at 7 under the bridge of the nose.

4. Continue working with the same thread to form the mouth.

   a. Reenter at 7 and exit at 8

   b. Pull the thread across the surface, enter at 9, and then exit at 3.

   c. Pull the thread until a smile appears. Reenter at 3 and exit at 7.

   d. Lock the stitch and cut the thread.

5. Add additional stitches to the mouth, following the entry and exit points illustrated in **Figure K**.

   a. Enter at 8 and exit at 10.

   b. Reenter at 10 and exit at 11.

   c. Reenter at 11 and exit at 12. Pull the thread to form the lips. Lock the stitch, exiting at 12.

   d. Reenter at 12 and exit at 13.

   e. Reenter at 13 and exit at 14.

   f. Reenter at 14 and exit at 15.

   g. Reenter at 15 and exit at 16.

   h. Lock the stitch and cut the thread.

6. To form one ear, follow the entry and exit points illustrated in **Figure L**.

   a. Pinch up a small ridge at an angle on the side of the head just below the eye line. Enter at 1 and exit at 17.

   b. Stitch back and forth underneath the ridge, between points 17 and 18. Pull the thread until an ear appears and exit at 18.

   c. Lock the stitch and return to 1.

   d. Lock the stitch and cut the thread.

7. Repeat step 6 to form an ear on the other side of the head.

8. To form the eyes and eyelids, follow the entry and exit points illustrated in **Figure M**.

   a. Enter at 1 and exit at 2.

   b. Pull the thread across the surface, enter at 19, and exit at 2. Pull the thread and lock the stitch at 2.

   c. Pinch up a narrow curved ridge over the left eye line. This will be the eyelid.

   d. Reenter at 2 and stitch back and forth under the eyelid ridge, exiting at 19.

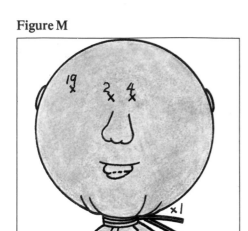

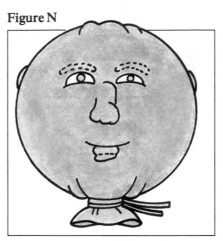

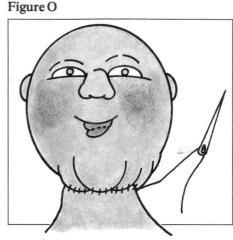

Figure P

Figure Q

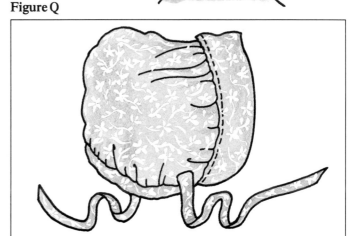

e. Reenter at 19 and exit at 2. Pull the thread gently and lock the stitch.

f. Reenter at 2 and exit at 4.

9. Repeat the procedures in step 8 on the right side of the face to form the other eye and eyelid.

10. To form Aunt Goldie's eyebrows, pinch up a ridge over one eyelid, even with the top of the nose, and stitch back and forth underneath the ridge (**Figure N**). Repeat on the other side of the face.

11. Paint the eyes using acrylic paint and a fine-tipped brush. First, paint the eye white and let the paint dry. Paint a blue iris in the center of each eye and add a darker blue or black pupil.

12. Add color to Aunt Goldie's cheeks and lips, using powdered cheek blusher.

Attaching the Head

Remove the string from around the neck, and center the head over the neck opening in the body. Whipstitch the head securely to the neck, as shown in **Figure O**.

Making the Bonnet

1. Pin the two Bonnet Brims right sides together and stitch the seam along the long curved edge, leaving the straight edge open. Clip the curves and turn the bonnet brim right side out. Press the seam allowances to the inside along the open edge.

2. Press a ¼-inch-wide hem to the wrong side of the Bonnet piece along the straight edge only. To make a casing for the elastic, turn the same edge under again, ½ inch. Topstitch close to

the inner edge leaving both ends open. Thread the length of elastic through the casing, and then stitch across the open ends of the casing to secure the elastic.

3. Gather the curved edge of the Bonnet piece, so that it matches the length of the straight Bonnet Brim edge. Adjust the gathers evenly, and baste over them to secure.

4. Insert the gathered edge of the bonnet between the pressed edges of the assembled brim (**Figure P**). Topstitch ¼ inch from the edge.

5. To make one tie, fold one Tie piece in half lengthwise, placing right sides together. Cut one end at an angle, and stitch the seam along the long edge and the angled short edge. Clip the corners and turn the tie right side out. Turn the seam allowance to the inside around the open edge, and press.

6. Make a second tie in the same manner.

7. Fold over the straight short end of one tie about 3 inches. Topstitch the folded end of the tie to the lower edge of the bonnet, near the brim on one side, as shown in **Figure Q**.

8. Follow the same procedures to attach the second tie to the opposite side of the bonnet.

Finishing

Place the wig on Aunt Goldie's head and glue or stitch in place. Put her bonnet on and tie a bow at the front. Aunt Goldie gets goose bumps rather easily, so dress her quickly. Don't forget the shawl – she won't go anywhere without it.

Materials

1 yard of red flannel
1 yard of black satin
½ yard of white cotton fabric for the bag lining
A bag of polyester fiberfill
One 2-inch-diameter white pompom
Two ¾-inch-diameter plastic eyes (We used the kind with moving eyeballs.)
One regular-weave flesh-tone nylon stocking, or one leg cut from the same type of pantyhose
2-foot length of thin wire for Santa's eyeglasses (optional)
12-inch length of white ¼-inch-diameter cotton cord
Cosmetic cheek blusher
Sprig of holly (optional)
Heavy-duty flesh-tone thread, regular sewing thread to match the fabrics; a long sharp needle; and white glue or hot-melt glue and a glue gun

Cutting the Pieces

1. Scale drawings for the Hat, Mitten, and Bag are provided in **Figure A**. Enlarge the scale drawings to make full-size patterns for each of these pieces.

2. Cut one Arm piece 12 x 44 inches from red flannel. If the flannel you purchased is not wide enough to accommodate the 44-inch length, cut two rectangles, each 12 x 22½ inches. Place them right sides together and stitch a seam along one 12-inch edge. Press the seam open. You should now have a 12 x 44-inch rectangle of fabric.

3. Cut the pieces listed here from the specified fabrics.

Red flannel: Hat – cut one
Black satin: Mitten – cut four
              Bag – cut two
White cotton: Bag Lining – cut two, using the same pattern that you used for the bag

Santa Card Holder

Santa's bag of goodies can hold more than toys for the little ones. Here's a cute way to let Santa help display all the beautiful cards of the holiday season. You could also fill Santa's bag with candy canes, pine cones, or any number of festive accessories. He is approximately 12 inches tall.

1 square = 1 inch

Figure A

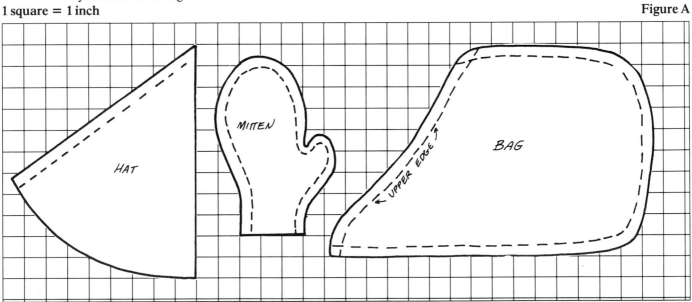

Figure B

Figure C

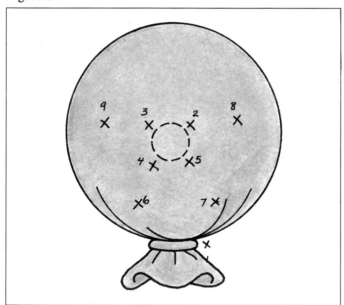

Figure D

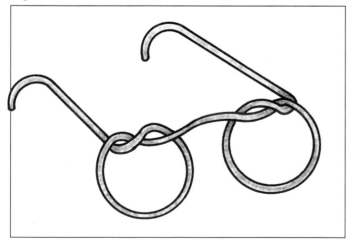

Making the Head

1. Tie the upper end of the nylon stocking in a knot, or wrap it tightly with heavy-duty thread, and trim off any excess hose about 1 inch above the knot. Cut across the hose approximately 9 inches below the knot; you will not need the lower portion for this project. Turn the hose so the knot is on the inside.

2. Stuff the hose with fiberfill until you have formed a round head about 18 inches in diameter. The knot on the inside will be the top of the head.

3. Gather the hose at the neck, and wrap it tightly with heavy-duty thread (**Figure B**). Cut off any excess hose about 1 inch below the neck.

4. Use a long sharp needle and one long strand of heavy-duty flesh-tone thread to form Santa's facial features. Follow the entry and exit points illustrated in **Figure C**.

   a. To form the nose, enter at point 1, where the hose is tied at the neck, guide the needle through the center of the head, and exit at 2. Sew a circle of basting stitches approximately ¾ inch in diameter, and exit at 3.

   b. Use the tip of the needle to carefully lift the fiberfill within the circle just enough to make a small bulge. Pull the thread until a round nose appears, and lock the stitch at the bridge of the nose, exiting at 2.

   c. To form the nostrils, reenter at 2 and exit at 4.

   d. Reenter ¼ inch above 4, on the nose, and exit at 3.

   e. Reenter at 3 and exit at 5.

   f. Reenter ¼ inch above 5 and exit at 2. Pull the thread until the nostrils appear, and lock the stitch at the bridge of the nose, exiting at 2.

5. Continue working with the same thread to form the eyes and mouth, following the entry and exit points illustrated in **Figure C**.

   a. To form the mouth, reenter at 2 and exit at 6.

   b. Pull the thread across the surface, enter at 7, and exit at 3. Pull the thread until a smile appears, and lock the stitch at the bridge of the nose, exiting at 3.

   c. To form the eyes, reenter at 3 and exit at 8.

   d. Pull the thread across the surface, enter at 2, exit at 9.

   e. Pull the thread across the surface, enter at 3, and exit at 2. Gently pull the thread until the closed eyes appear. Lock the stitch at the bridge of the nose, exiting at 2.

   f. Reenter at 2 and exit at 1. Lock the stitch and then cut the thread.

6. Glue a plastic eye to each side of the bridge of Santa's nose, over the eye lines.

7. Glue a fluffy white fiberfill eyebrow above each eye.

8. Apply cosmetic cheek blusher to the tip of Santa's pudgy little nose, and to his cheeks.

9. If you want your Santa to wear eyeglasses, simply bend and twist the length of thin wire, as shown in **Figure D**. Glue or tack the glasses to Santa's face.

Making the Arms

Note: All seams are ½ inch wide unless otherwise specified in the instructions. Santa's body consists of a stuffed-flannel arm tube, with a stuffed-satin mitten attached to each end.

Figure I

1. Fold the flannel Arm piece in half lengthwise, placing right sides together. Stitch the seam along the long edge only, leaving the two short ends open and unstitched. Turn the tube right side out, and press the seam allowances to the inside around the two short open edges. Stuff the tube with fiberfill.

2. To make one mitten, place two Mitten pieces right sides together. Stitch the seam all the way around the long contoured edge, leaving the straight short wrist edge open and unstitched (**Figure E**). Clip the curves and the inside corner at the base of the thumb, and turn the mitten right side out. Stuff the mitten with fiberfill.

3. Make a second mitten in the same manner, using the two remaining Mitten pieces.

4. Insert the wrist portion of one mitten inside one open end of the arm tube. Turn the mitten so the thumb is pointing upward, and the long seam in the arm tube is at the bottom. Whipstitch around the wrist two times to secure the assembly. Attach the remaining mitten to the opposite end of the arm tube in the same manner, making sure that both thumbs point in the same direction.

5. Glue a 3- or 4-inch-wide fiberfill cuff around each end of the arm tube, covering the wrist stitches.

Making the Hat

1. Fold the Hat piece along the "place on fold" line, right sides together. Stitch the seam along the long straight edge only, leaving the lower edge open and unstitched (**Figure F**).

2. Turn the hat right side out and press the seam allowance to the inside around the open lower edge. Glue or stitch the hem in place. Stuff the hat with fiberfill, leaving the tip unstuffed. Glue or tack the white pompom to the tip of the hat.

3. Fold the upper portion of the hat to one side, and glue or tack the pompom to the side of the hat. Glue a 2- or 3-inch border of fiberfill around the bottom of the hat (**Figure G**).

Assembly

1. Place the arm assembly on a flat surface, with the thumbs pointing upward, and mark the center of the tube. Place Santa's head at the center point, and whipstitch the head to the arm tube securely, as shown in **Figure H**. This seam will be covered by hair and beard, and the stitches won't show.

2. Now that Santa is more or less in one piece, it will be easier to cover his chubby face with fluffy white whiskers and mustache. To form the mustache, glue a long, billowy piece of fiberfill under each soft-sculpted nostril.

Figure J

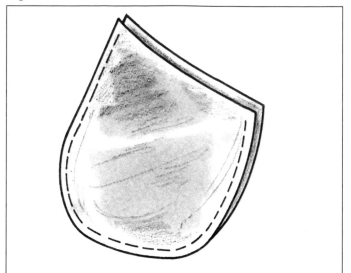

Figure K

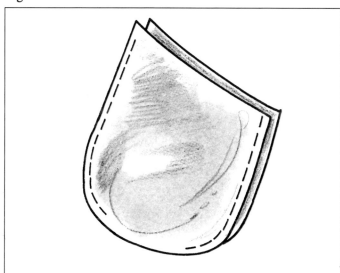

Figure L

Figure M

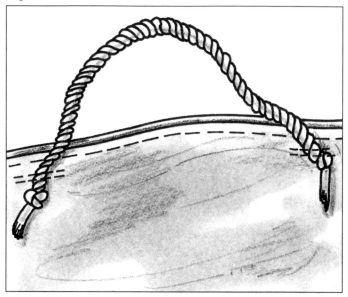

3. To make the beard, form a large, cloudlike piece of fiberfill, and glue it to Santa's face just beneath his lower lip.

4. Glue or whipstitch Santa's hat to his head. To form his hair, glue fiberfill to the head around the lower edge of the hat.

5. Refer to **Figure I** as you fold Santa's arms into a position that will allow him to hold his goodie-filled bag over one shoulder. Tack the arms in place.

6. You can add an additional decorative touch to your Santa by glueing a sprig of holly to the border of his hat.

Making the Goodie Bag

1. Place the two satin Bag pieces right sides together and stitch the seam all the way around the long contoured edge, leaving the angled upper edge open and unstitched (**Figure J**). Clip the curves, press the seam open, turn the bag right side out.

2. Place the two Bag Lining pieces right sides together and stitch as you did the bag, but leave a 3-inch opening at the bottom (**Figure K**). Clip the curves, press the seam open, and press the seam allowances to the wrong side of the fabric along each side of the opening at the bottom. Leave the bag lining wrong side out.

3. To join the bag and lining, slip the satin bag down inside the lining so the upper raw edges of the two are even. The two bags should now be right sides together. Stitch the two layers together around the entire upper edge (**Figure L**). To turn the assembly right side out, pull the satin bag through the opening at the bottom of the lining and continue to pull until the lining turns itself right side out. Whipstitch the opening edges together at the bottom of the lining, and then push it down inside the bag. Press the upper seam flat, and then gently press the entire bag.

4. Tie a knot near each end of the cotton cord, so it won't ravel, and stitch the cord to the upper edges of the bag to form a strap, as shown in **Figure M**.

5. Slip the cord over Santa's hands. You may wish to tack or glue the cord in place. Santa can be used effectively on a flat surface such as a table or mantel, with his goodie bag stretched out behind him. Merry Christmas!

Materials

Note: There are several variations that can be made in this project, so feel free to be as creative as you like. You probably have most of the materials on hand, but if you do not, visit your local thrift shop for some terrific bargains.

An oval washtub, approximately 22 inches long and 12 inches wide (We used a copper tub with wooden handles.)

3 yards of muslin

Two pairs of flesh-tone nylon pantyhose

Three pairs of flesh-tone knee-high hose

Six bags of polyester fiberfill

Acrylic paints in white, blue, black, and brown; and an artist's fine-tipped paint brush

A long sharp needle; regular sewing thread; and heavy-duty flesh-tone thread

White glue or hot-melt glue and a glue gun

1-yard length of string

For the butcher:
Boy's size 8 long-sleeved plaid shirt
Small bib apron
Wig (We used a light brown wig.)
Small white butcher's cap
Wooden meat-tenderizing mallet

For the baker:
Boy's size 8 long-sleeved turtleneck sweater
Long, bushy wig (We used a shoulder-length brown wig.)
Small woven basket, approximately 6 inches in diameter
Large calico napkin to line the bread basket
Two artificial dinner rolls (You can use real dinner rolls if you first dry them in the oven and then apply shellac.)
Chef's hat
Rolling pin

For the candlestick maker:
Boy's size 8 long-sleeved shirt
Long bushy wig (We used a shoulder-length gray wig.)
Wooden candlestick holder and candle

Cutting the Pieces

Cut the Body pieces listed here from muslin:

Torso – cut four, each 15 x 21 inches
            cut two, each 17 x 21 inches
Arm – cut six, each 9 x 12 inches

THE BUTCHER
Making the Torso and Arms

Note: All seams are ½ inch wide unless otherwise specified in the instructions.

1. Shape the neck and shoulder edges of two of the 15 x 21-inch Torso pieces, as shown in **Figure A**.

2. Place the two Torso pieces together and stitch the seam along each shoulder and side edge, leaving the neck and lower edges open. Leave arm openings, as shown in **Figure B**.

3. To make one arm, fold one Arm piece in half lengthwise

Three Men in a Tub

Rub-a-dub-dub! They're all here: the butcher, the baker and the candlestick maker. Let this children's verse come to whimsical life as a unique kitchen decoration or child's conversation piece. The overall dimensions are approximately 22 x 20 inches.

Figure A

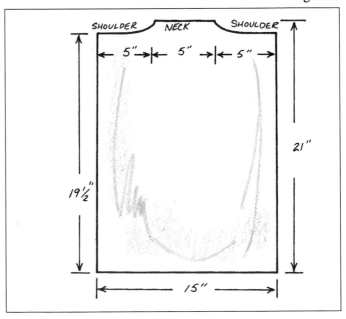

Figure B

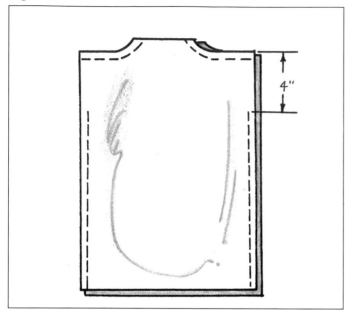

Figure C

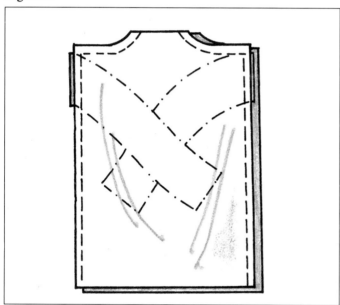

Figure D

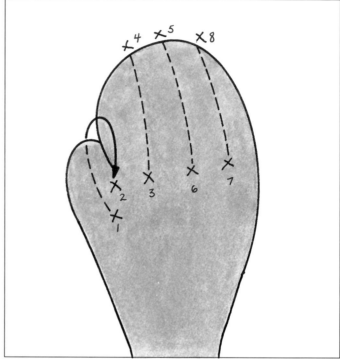

and stitch the seam along the long edge, leaving the two short edges open. Turn the arm right side out.

4. Make a second arm in the same manner. The hands will be added later.

5. The torso should still be wrong side out. Insert one arm inside and pin the open shoulder edge of the arm to one armhole edge of the torso. Pin the second arm in place in the same manner, and stitch the two Torso pieces together along each arm hole, with the arms sandwiched between, as shown in **Figure C.** Turn the torso right side out and press the seam allowances to the inside around the lower edge and neck edge, and around the lower arm edges.

6. Stuff the torso with fiberfill, leaving 1 inch unstuffed at the bottom, and whipstitch the lower edges together. Stuff the arms as well, but do not stitch the ends together.

Making the Hands

1. To make one hand, lightly stuff the foot portion of one knee-high stocking until it is a ball approximately 8 inches in diameter. Tie the hose in a knot. This will be the wrist. Make a second hand in the same manner, keeping them as equal in size and shape as possible.

2. To soft-sculpt the fingers, follow the entry and exit points illustrated in **Figure D**, using a long sharp needle and heavy-duty flesh-tone thread.

   a. Flatten one hand slightly, and insert the needle on the back of the hand, 3½ inches from the wrist end, at point 1. Push the needle straight through the hand and exit on the palm side. This will be the base of the thumb.

   b. Pinch up a ridge on the thumb side of the hand. Wrap the thread around what will be the end of the thumb, enter at 2 on the back, and exit at 1 on the palm side.

   c. Pull the thread and lock the stitch. Reenter at 1 and exit at 3.

   d. Stitch up and down through the hand along the dotted line between 3 and 4.

   e. Enter at 4 and exit at point 5. Pull the thread and lock the stitch securely.

   f. To form the last three fingers, repeat the procedures in steps d and e, stitching between 5 and 6 and then between 7 and 8.

   g. Lock the last stitch and cut the thread.

3. Repeat the procedures in step 2 to soft-sculpt the fingers on the remaining hand.

4. Trim the excess hose, slip the tied wrist end of one hand inside the open lower end of one arm, and securely whipstitch the hand in place. Attach the remaining hand to the other arm in the same manner.

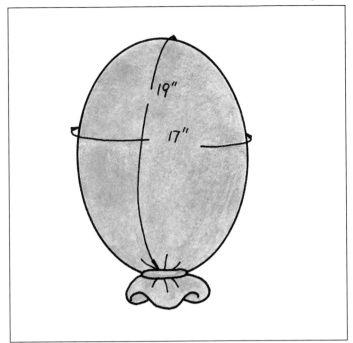

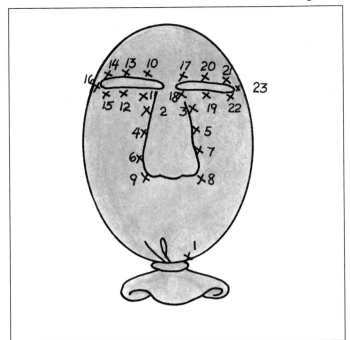

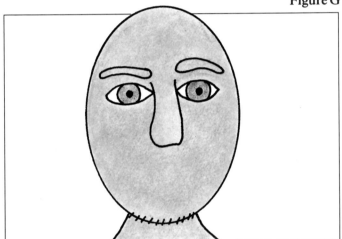

Making the Head

1. To form the head, tie a knot at the panty line of one leg of nylon pantyhose. Cut across the hose 1 inch above the knot. Cut again 14 inches below the knot. Turn the hose so the knot is on the inside.

2. Stuff generous amounts of fiberfill inside the hose, manipulating the shape until a head is formed (**Figure E**). The completed head should be approximately 19 inches in circumference lengthwise and 17 inches in circumference widthwise, as shown in **Figure E**. Tie the hose loosely at the neck, using a short length of string.

3. To soft-sculpt the facial features, follow the entry and exit points illustrated in **Figure F**. As you work, pull the thread tight to create more defined facial features, or less tight to create softer facial features.

   a. To form the nose, enter at 1 where the hose is knotted at the neck. Push the needle through the center of the head and exit at 2.

   b. Pinch up a vertical ridge in the center of the face, approximately ¾ inch wide. Reenter at 2, push the needle under the ridge, and exit at 3.

   c. Reenter at 3, and continue to stitch back and forth underneath the ridge between points 4, 5, 6, and 7. Exit at 7.

   d. Pull the thread across the surface, enter at 8, and exit at point 6.

   e. Pull the thread across the surface again, enter at 9, and exit at 3.

   f. Pull the thread and lock the stitch at 3.

4. To form the eyebrows, continue working with the same length of thread.

   a. Reenter at 3 and exit at 10. Pinch up a narrow, horizontal ridge, approximately 2 inches long. Reenter at 10, push the needle under the ridge, and exit at 11.

   b. Stitch back and forth underneath the eyebrow ridge, passing through points 12, 13, 14, and 15. Exit at 15.

   c. Enter at 16 and exit at 17. Lock the stitch.

   d. The left eyebrow is complete. Follow the procedures in steps a through c to form the right eyebrow, using the corresponding numbers on the right side of the face. When you have completed the eyebrows, lock the stitch and cut the thread.

5. Paint the eyes using acrylic paint and a fine-tipped brush. First, paint the eyes white and let the paint dry. Paint a brown iris in the center of each eye, and a darker brown or black pupil in the center of each iris (**Figure G**).

Finishing

1. Insert the tied neck portion of the head inside the neck opening of the torso. Whipstitch the head securely to the neck, as shown in **Figure G**.

Figure H

Figure J

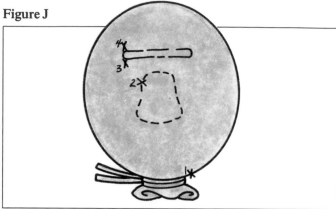

Figure K

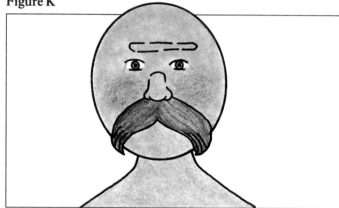

Figure I

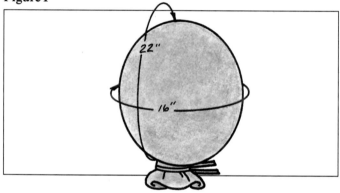

2. To make the mustache, we cut off a portion of the wig near the back, and glued the locks underneath the nose. To do so, first place the wig on the head and arrange it to your satisfaction. Determine where hair will be missed least, remove the wig, and cut off a couple of locks, each about 2 inches long. Gather one end of each lock and glue the loose hairs together. When the glue has dried, apply additional glue and attach the locks to the face, as shown in **Figure H**.

3. Position the butcher's cap on the center of the head and glue or stitch it in place.

4. Dress the butcher in his shirt and bib apron and set him aside for now.

THE BAKER
Making the Body

The baker, as one might suspect, is the plumpest of the three, so use the 17 x 21-inch Torso pieces. To assemble the baker's body, follow the same procedures as you did for the butcher's, adding considerably more stuffing to the torso. The baker's arms and hands are made in the same manner as the butcher's.

Making the Head

1. Follow the same basic procedures as you did to form the butcher's head. The baker's head should be approximately 22 inches in circumference lengthwise and 16 inches in circumference widthwise, as shown in **Figure I**.

2. To soft-sculpt the facial features, follow the entry and exit points illustrated in **Figure J**.

    a. The nose is a large, pear-shaped outline of stitches. To form the nose, enter at 1 where the hose is knotted at the neck. Push the needle through the center of the head and exit at 2.

    b. Begin at 2 and sew a pear-shaped outline of stitches so that the bridge of the nose is approximately 3 inches wide and the lower portion is approximately 4 inches wide, returning to and exiting at 2. Pull the thread to form the nose, and gently lift fiberfill within the nose outline. Lock the stitch at 2.

    c. The baker has one long forehead wrinkle. To form the wrinkle, reenter at 2 and exit at 3. Pinch up a horizontal ridge, approximately ¼ inch wide. Push the needle under the ridge and exit at 4.

    d. Stitch back and forth underneath the ridge until the eyebrow is approximately 3 inches long. Lock the stitch and cut the thread.

3. Paint the eyes in the same manner as you did the butcher's.

4. Attach the head to the body in the same manner as you did the butcher's.

5. The baker's hair and mustache are added in basically the same manner as the butcher's. The only difference is that we cut the mustache from the top of the wig, leaving the poor guy bald on top. His mustache is approximately 6 inches wide and 4 inches long. Refer to **Figure K** as you glue the mustache underneath the nose.

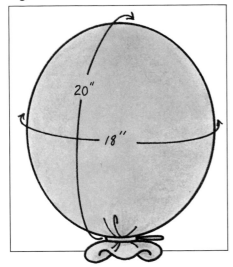

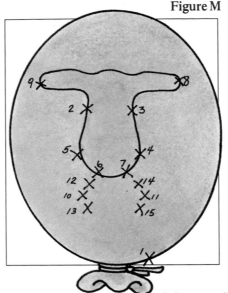

Finishing

Dress the baker in his turtleneck sweater. If necessary, you can cut a slit down the back of the neck, and then stitch it closed after you've pulled the sweater over his head. Position the chef's hat on the center of his bald head and glue or stitch it in place securely.

THE CANDLESTICK MAKER
Making the Body

To make the candlestick maker's torso, follow the procedures for making the butcher's torso, using the same measurements. Make the arms in the same manner as you did the butcher's and baker's. To assemble the body, follow the same procedures as you did for the butcher's. His hands are made in the same manner as the butcher's and baker's.

Making the Head

1. Follow the same basic procedures as you did to form the first two heads, making this one approximately 20 inches in circumference lengthwise and 18 inches in circumference widthwise, as shown in **Figure L**.

2. To soft-sculpt the facial features, follow the entry and exit points illustrated in **Figure M**.

  a. To form the nose, enter at 1, push the needle through the center of the head, and exit at 2.

  b. Pinch up a vertical nose ridge approximately 1 inch wide. Reenter at 2, push the needle under the ridge, and exit at 3.

  c. Stitch back and forth underneath the ridge as you did for the butcher, until the nose is approximately 2½ inches long, and exit at 4. Reenter at 4, push the needle under the nose ridge, and exit at 5. Lock the stitch. Reenter at 5 and exit at 7. Reenter at 7 and exit at 5. Reenter at 5 and exit at 6. Reenter at 6 and exit at 4. Lock the stitch at 4.

  d. To form the eyebrow ridge, reenter at 4 and exit at 8.

  e. Pinch up a horizontal ridge, approximately ½ inch wide. Stitch back and forth underneath the ridge until

it is approximatley 4 inches long, and exit at 9. Pull the thread and lock the stitch at 9.

  f. Reenter at 9 and exit at 3.

  g. To form the mouth, reenter at 3, and exit at 10. Pull the thread across the surface, enter at 11, and exit at 12.

  h. Reenter at 12 and exit at 13.

  i. Reenter at 13 and exit at 14.

  j. Reenter at 14 and exit at 15. Pull the thread and lock the stitch at 15.

  k. Reenter at 15 and exit at 1. Lock the stitch securely and cut the thread.

3. Paint the eyes, using white and blue acrylic paints.

4. Attach the head to the body in the same manner as you did his partners'.

5. The candlestick maker's hair and beard are added in basically the same manner as his friends'. We cut the beard from the back of the wig. It measures approximately 8 inches wide and 4 inches long. Refer to **Figure N** as you glue the beard in place on his face.

6. Dress the candlestick maker in his slong-sleeved shirt.

FINAL ASSEMBLY

1. Pad the bottom of the washtub with fiberfill to make sure the guys can see over the top of the tub. Place the butcher at one end of the tub, the baker next to him, and the candlestick maker at the other end, as shown in **Figure O**.

2. Place the meat tenderizer in the butcher's exposed hand, wrap the fingers snugly around the handle, and either glue or stitch the fingers together.

3. Spread a layer of fiberfill in the bottom of the woven basket, place the calico napkin on top, and place the dinner rolls in the basket.

4. Place the basket in the baker's hands and glue the hands to the basket.

5. Place the candle in the candlestick holder and place the holder in the candlestick maker's exposed hand. Glue or stitch the fingers around the holder. **Note:** Cut off the wick of the candle to reduce the risk of fire hazard.

6. Spread any leftover fiberfill throughout the tub.

Bunny Baby

The tiny tot who has a soft and cuddly bunny baby to curl up with at nap time is lucky indeed. This project is simple to make and can be stitched up in no time. What better or easier way to please that special little one. Bunny baby is about 12 inches tall.

Materials

½ yard of soft flannel or fleece for the sleeper and hood, in the color of your choice
6-inch square of white flannel for the blanket.
One nylon knee-high stocking for the head
1½-inch-diameter white pompom for the tail
½ yard of 1-inch-wide ribbon for the bow, in a color to coordinate with the flannel
Small quantity of polyester fiberfill
Long sharp needle and heavy-duty flesh-tone thread
Cosmetic cheek blusher
Black fabric paint or a black medium-point permanent marker

Cutting the Pieces

1. Scale drawings for the Sleeper, Hood, and Ear patterns are provided in **Figure A**. Enlarge the scale drawings to make full-size patterns.
2. Cut the following pieces from flannel:

Sleeper – cut two
Hood – cut two
Ear – cut four

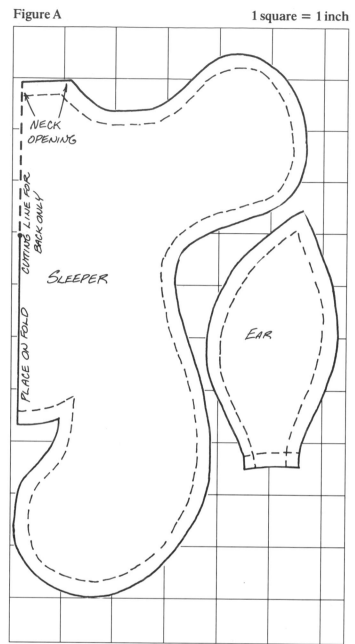

Figure A   1 square = 1 inch

NECK OPENING

CUTTING LINE FOR BACK ONLY

PLACE ON FOLD

SLEEPER

EAR

Making the Body

Note: All seams are ¼ inch wide unless otherwise specified in the instructions.

1. Place the two Sleeper pieces right sides together and stitch the seam all the way around the edge, leaving the neck open (**Figure B**). Clip the curves and corners and press the seam open. Turn the sleeper right side out and stuff with fiberfill.

2. Cut an ear slit in each Hood piece where indicated on the scale drawing. Place the Hood pieces right sides together, matching the notches. Stitch the center back and front seams, leaving the curved front and neck edges open, as shown in **Figure C**. Clip the curves and press the seams open.

3. To make one ear, place two Ear pieces right sides together and stitch a continuous seam along the two curved edges,

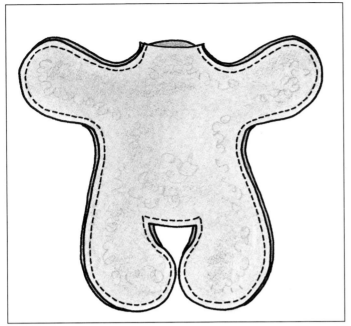

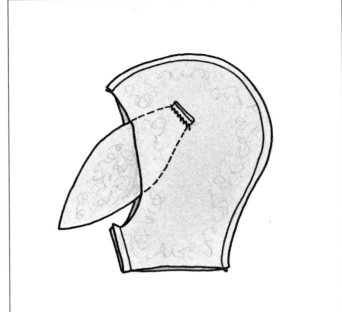

Figure C

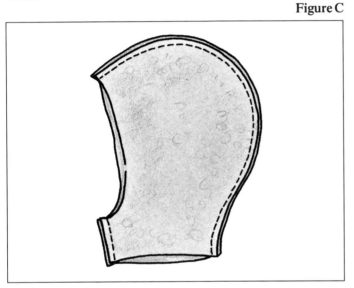

leaving the straight lower edge open. Clip the curves and turn the ear right side out. Press gently.

4. Make a second ear in the same manner.

5. The hood should still be wrong side out. Insert the open end of one ear into the slit in one side of the hood, as shown in **Figure D**. Whipstitch the ear in place on the wrong side of the hood. Follow the same procedures to attach the second ear to the opposite side of the hood.

6. Turn the hood right side out.

Making the Head

1. Tie a knot at the ankle of the knee-high stocking. Turn the hose so the knot is on the inside. Stuff the hose with fiberfill until the head is approximately 3½ inches in diameter. Tie the hose in a knot at the neck (**Figure E**), and trim the excess hose below the neck knot.

2. Follow the entry and exit points illustrated in **Figure F** to sculpt the facial features. Use a long sharp needle and heavy-duty flesh-tone thread.

   a. Enter at 1, push the needle through the center of the head, and exit at 2. To form the nose, sew a circle of basting stitches no larger than a quarter, exiting at 3.

   b. Use the tip of the needle to very carefully lift the fiberfill within the circle just enough to make a small bulge. Gently pull the thread until a small round nose appears. Lock the stitch and exit at 2.

   c. To form the eye lines, pull the thread across the surface approximately 1 inch, enter at 4, and exit at 3.

   d. Pull the thread across the surface approximately 1 inch, enter at 5, and exit at 2. Pull the thread gently to form the eyes. Lock the stitch at 2.

   e. To form the mouth, reenter at 2 and exit at 6.

   f. Pull the thread across the surface approximately 1 inch, enter at 7, and exit at 2. Pull the thread gently to form the mouth.

   g. Lock the stitch and cut the thread.

Figure F

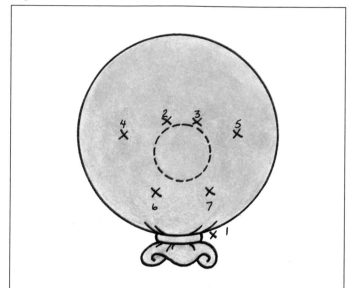

Figure G

Figure H

Figure I

3. Paint the eyes and eyebrows (**Figure G**), using black fabric paint or a permanent marker. Use cosmetic cheek blusher to add color to the nose, cheeks, and mouth, and brush a little blusher on the front of each ear.

Assembly

1. Press the seam allowance to the inside of the hood around the circular open front edge. Insert the head and blind stitch it in place around the front opening, using small invisible stitches (**Figure H**).

2. Press the seam allowance to the inside around the neck opening of the sleeper. Insert the neck edge of the hood and whipstitch around the neck to secure it. Wrap the ribbon around the bunny's neck and tie a bow at the front. Glue the pompom to the back side as a tail. Pink the edges of the white flannel, or stitch a narrow hem. Fold one arm over the chest and stitch it in place. Slip the flannel blanket underneath the arm as Bunny's security blanket.

Materials

For *each* male elf, you'll need the following:
One leg of nurse's white pantyhose
16 x 25-inch piece of dark green felt
5 x 7-inch piece of bright yellow felt
4 x 8-inch piece of white felt
7 x 10-inch piece of black felt
7 x 9-inch piece of red felt
Three red pompoms, each ½ inch in diameter
¾ yard of tiny gold tinsel or very narrow gold braid (optional)
Twelve red sequins, each ¼ inch in diameter (optional)
One strip of fake fur fabric, with long fur, for the beard (If you prefer, you can use polyester fiberfill.)
Cosmetic cheek blusher; a small quantity of polyester fiberfill; heavy-duty thread in yellow, white, and green; a long sharp needle; white glue or hot-melt glue and a glue gun
Weights: One pound or so of marbles, smooth clean stones, fishing weights, or something similar
Four chenille stems (large pipe cleaners) in any color

For *each* female elf, you'll need:
One leg of nurse's white pantyhose
6-inch-square piece of dark green felt
6 x 14-inch piece of red felt
7 x 12-inch piece of white felt
4 x 6-inch piece of yellow felt
One skein of yellow/gold rug yarn
Three red pompoms
¾ yard of tiny red tinsel or very narrow braid (optional)
12-inch length of tiny gold tinsel or very narrow braid (optional)
Twelve red sequins, each ¼ inch in diameter (optional)
½ yard of green grosgrain ribbon, ⅜ inch wide
Cosmetic cheek blusher; a small quantity of polyester fiberfill; heavy-duty thread in green and white; a long sharp needle; white glue or hot-melt glue and a glue gun
Weights: One pound or so of marbles, smooth clean stones, fishing weights, or something similar
Four chenille stems of any color

Cutting the Pieces

1. Scale drawings for the Pants, Hat, Collar, Skirt, Belt, Beanbag, Beanbag Bottom, Shirt, and Shoe are provided in **Figure A**. Enlarge the drawings to make full-size patterns.

2. Full-size patterns for the Ear, Hand, Sleeve, and Belt Buckle are provided in **Figure B**. Trace the patterns onto tracing or pattern paper.

3. Cut the pieces as listed here from the specified fabrics.

For one male elf:

Yellow felt: Collar – cut one
          Buckle – cut one
Green felt: Shirt – cut two
        Sleeve – cut two
        Shoe – cut four
        Bean Bag – cut two
        Bean Bag Bottom – cut one

Elf Stocking Holders

These elves can be used as holiday decorations just about anywhere in the house, but they do a great job of holding stockings over the fireplace – and you don't have to drive a nail into your lovely woodwork! Their bottoms are weighted so they'll sit solidly in whatever position you place them, and their legs and arms contain chenille stems so they'll hold the weight of a fully loaded stocking.

Red felt: Hat – cut one
       Belt – cut one
Black felt: Pants – cut two
White felt: Hand – cut four
       Ear – cut two

For one female elf:

Yellow felt: Hand – cut four
Green felt: Shoe – cut four
       Collar – cut one
       Beanbag – cut two
       Beanbag Bottom – cut one
Red felt: Skirt – cut one
      Hat – cut one
White felt: Ear – cut two
       Pants – cut two
Rug yarn: Hair – cut forty-two 9-inch strands

1 square = 1 inch

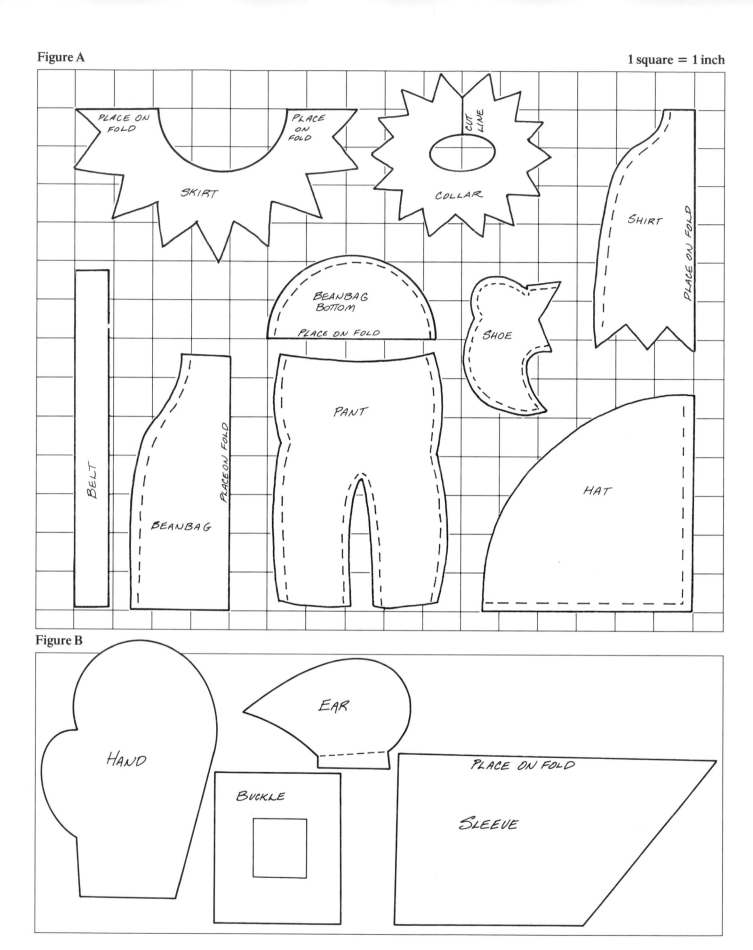

Figure B

Figure C

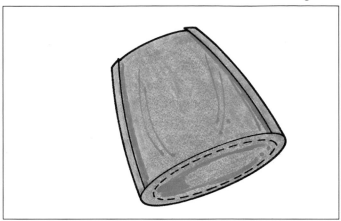

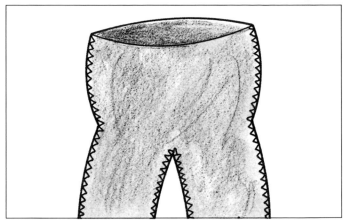

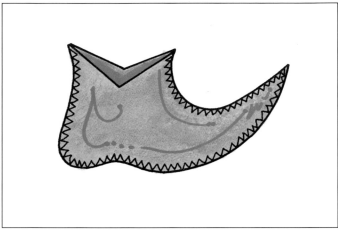

THE MALE ELF

The elf's body is a simple beanbag that contains the weights. The head, legs and feet, arms and hands, and tunic are made separately and glued or stitched to the weighted bag.

Making the Beanbag

1. Place the two Beanbag pieces together and stitch the two side seams as indicated on the scale drawing, using a ¼-inch-wide seam. Press the seams open, and leave the pieces turned wrong side out. Place the Beanbag Bottom piece inside the lower (large) open edge of this assembly, and stitch it in place (**Figure C**). Turn the beanbag right side out.

2. Fill the beanbag about half full of marbles or whatever you have chosen for weights. Stuff the upper half with fiberfill.

Making the Legs and Feet

Note: We made outside seams on most of the clothing pieces. It's easier that way, and if you will use a contrasting thread color and a small zigzag stitch to sew the seams, it will add to the holiday look.

1. The elf doesn't really have legs – just stuffed pants! Place the two Pants pieces together and stitch the side and inner leg seams, using a small zigzag stitch (**Figure D**).

2. The elf doesn't really have feet, either – just stuffed shoes! Place two of the Shoe pieces together and stitch the seam all the way along the long contoured edge (**Figure E**), using a zigzag stitch. Leave the upper V-shaped edge open and unstitched as shown. Stitch the remaining two Shoe pieces together in the same manner.

3. Stuff the two shoes lightly with fiberfill.

4. Chenille stems provide strength in the legs and feet. Bend a small loop at the end of one chenille stem, and insert the looped end into one of the shoes, all the way down to the toe. Bend the stem so it extends straight up out of the top of the shoe. Add fiberfill around it until the shoe is tightly stuffed. Bend a loop at the end of a second stem, insert it into the remaining shoe, and add stuffing.

5. Slip the open lower end of one pant leg down over the chenille stem that extends from one of the shoes (**Figure F**). Pull the pant leg down until you can tuck it into the shoe top, and glue the shoe and pant leg together. Do the same with the remaining shoe and the other pant leg. Now stuff each pant leg with fiberfill, working the stuffing in around the stem and keeping the stem in the center. Stuff to the top of the legs only – do not stuff the top of the pants above the crotch. Twist the upper ends of the two chenille stems together, just above the crotch. Twist the excess portion of the chenille stems around each other, or cut off the excess.

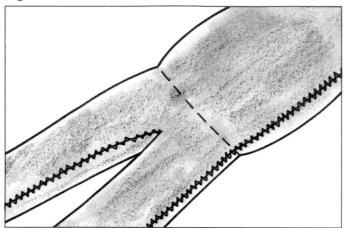

Figure I

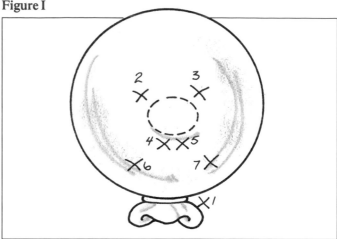

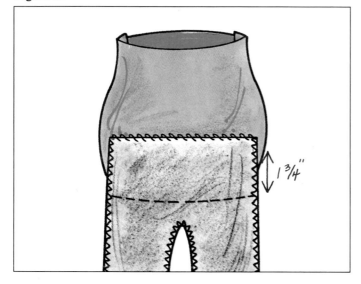

6. Run a line of straight machine stitches across the pants, just above the crotch (**Figure G**), through both the front and back layers.

7. Whipstitch the aligned upper edges of the pants to the beanbag, about 1¾ inches from the beanbag bottom, as shown in **Figure H**.

8. Glue or whipstitch a red pompom to the tip of each shoe. If you want, glue a length of gold tinsel or braid around the top of each shoe.

Making the Head

1. Tie a knot at the ankle of a stocking. Cut off the foot portion about 1 inch below the knot. Turn the hose so the knot is on the inside. Stuff the hose with fiberfill until the head is approximately 3 inches in diameter. Tie the hose in a knot at the neck, and trim the excess hose below the knot.

2. Follow the entry and exit points illustrated in **Figure I** to sculpt the facial features. Use a long sharp needle and heavy-duty white thread.

    a. To form the nose, enter at 1 and exit at 2. Sew a clockwise circle of basting stitches approximately 1 inch in diameter, and exit at 3.

    b. Use the tip of the needle to carefully lift the fiberfill within the circle enough to make a small bulge. Gently pull the thread until a little round nose appears. Lock the stitch, reenter at 3, and exit at 2.

    c. To form the nostrils, reenter at 2 and exit at 4.

    d. Reenter ¼ inch above 4 and exit at 3.

    e. Reenter at 3 and exit at 5.

    f. Reenter ¼ inch above 5 and exit at 2. Lock the stitch.

3. To form the mouth, continue working with the same length of thread.

    a. Reenter at 2 and exit at 6.

    b. Pull the thread across the surface, enter at 7, and exit at point 2.

    c. Gently pull the thread until a smile appears. Lock the stitch at 2.

    d. Reenter at 2 and exit at 1. Lock the stitch at 1 and cut the thread.

4. We didn't forget the eyes...the elves' eyes won't show.

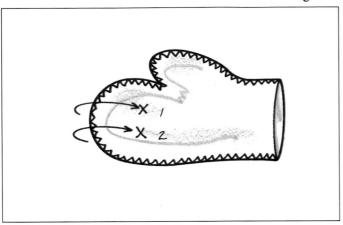

Figure L

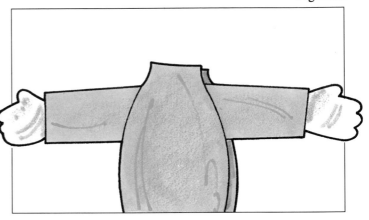

Making the Ears and Hat

1. Glue an ear to each side of the head, as shown in **Figure J**. Fold the ear tab under, and glue the tab to the side of the head, so the ear will stick out.

2. Cut a small strip of fake fur, or use fiberfill, and glue it to the face below the mouth as a beard.

3. Fold the Hat piece in half and stitch the seam (this is a normal, inside seam) along the long straight edge. Leave the lower curved edge open and unstitched. Turn the hat right side out.

4. Place the hat over the elf's head, and pull it down to his nose. Glue it in place. Glue a red pompom to the tip of the hat, bend the tip over to one side, and glue it to the hat. Glue gold tinsel or braid around the lower edge of the hat (optional).

5. Use the cosmetic blusher to add a spot of color to each cheek and each ear. You may wish to vary the facial features if you make additional male elves. We made one with no mouth, and gave him extra whiskers.

Making the Hands and Shirt

1. Place two Hand pieces together and stitch all the way around the long contoured edge, using a narrow zigzag stitch. Leave the straight wrist edge open and unstitched. Stuff the hand lightly with fiberfill. Use the two remaining Hand pieces to make a second hand.

2. We soft-sculpted fingers on each hand. To do this, use heavy-duty white thread and a long sharp needle, and follow the entry and exit points illustrated in **Figure K**.

   a. Enter on one side of the hand at point 1 (this will be the palm side of the hand). Push the needle straight through the hand and exit at point 1 on the back.

   b. Wrap the thread around the end of the hand, enter at 1 on the palm side, and exit at 1 on the back. Pull the thread gently to form a finger, and lock the stitch at 1.

   c. Reenter at 1 and exit at 2 on the palm side. Reenter at 2 and exit at 2 on the back.

   d. Wrap the thread around the end of the hand, enter at 2 on the palm side, and exit at 2 on the back. Pull the thread gently to form the finger, and lock the stitch at point 2. Cut the thread.

   e. Repeat the procedures in steps a through d to sculpt the fingers on the remaining hand.

3. Fold one of the Sleeve pieces in half wrong sides together along the "place on fold" line. Use a narrow zigzag stitch to sew the seam along the edge opposite the fold.

4. Bend a loop at one end of a chenille stem, and insert the looped end into one of the hands. Add a little extra stuffing around the stem, and whipstitch the open wrist edges together to hold the stem in place.

5. Insert the opposite end of the stem into one open end of the stitched sleeve (**Figure L**). Push the hand all the way up to the sleeve edge, and insert the wrist edge of the hand into the sleeve slightly. Glue the hand and sleeve together at the wrist and, if you want, glue a length of gold tinsel or braid around the wrist.

6. Work from the remaining open end of the sleeve, and bend the stem in a zigzag pattern inside the sleeve, so it does not extend out the open end.

7. Repeat the procedures in steps 3 through 6 to assemble the remaining hand and sleeve.

8. Place one of the Shirt pieces on a flat surface. Place the two sleeve/hand assemblies on top, as shown in **Figure M**, overlapping the sleeve and shirt edges by about ¼ inch. Be sure you have the sleeves turned so that both thumbs are pointing upward. Place the remaining Shirt piece on top, and pin the pieces together along each long side edge. Stitch the side seams, using a narrow zigzag stitch. Be sure to catch the sleeves in the seams.

Figure N

Making the Beanbag

Use the green felt Beanbag and Beanbag Bottom pieces for the female elf. Assemble and stuff the beanbag as you did for the male.

Making the Legs and Feet

Use the white felt Pants pieces and the green felt Shoe pieces for the female elf. Follow the same assembly instructions as you did for the male. Glue red tinsel or narrow braid around the tops of the shoes (optional).

Making the Head

Follow the same instructions as you did for the male elf's head. Cut and attach the ears as you did for the male. Use cosmetic blusher to create spots of color for the female elf's cheeks and ears.

Making the Hair and Hat

1. Divide the forty-two strands of rug yarn into two groups of twenty-one strands. Each of the groups will become one braid. Tie one group together at one end. Separate the strands into three equal parts, seven strands to a part. Braid the strands and tie them together at the end of the braid, using a 9-inch length of green grosgrain ribbon. Make the second braid as you did the first. Glue or whipstitch one braid to the female elf's head, placing the upper end just in front of and slightly above the top of one ear. Attach the remaining braid to the opposite side of the head.

2. Make the female elf's hat in the same manner as you did the male's. Use red tinsel or braid around the lower edge of the hat (optional). Attach a red pompom to the tip of the hat. Glue the hat to the elf's head, so that it covers the upper ends of the braids and comes down to about her nose.

Making the Shirt and Collar

Use the same patterns and cut the shirt and sleeves from white felt, and the collar from green felt. Cut the hands from yellow felt. Assemble them in the same manner, but use red tinsel or braid around the female's wrists. Slip the shirt assembly over the beanbag, and attach the head in the same manner as you did the male's.

Making the Skirt

Slip the skirt over the elf's head. The center opening should be large enough to allow you to do this, but if it's not, just cut the skirt at one point from the outer to the inner edge, and wrap it around her. The skirt will cover the bottom of the shirt. Glue the skirt in place, and glue a length of gold tinsel or braid around the waist edge of the skirt.

Finishing

The female elf has no belt. We positioned her so she will sit upright at the edge of the mantel, with her legs crossed in a lady-elf-like fashion (Figure N). Cross one foot over the other – there's no need to glue them together. You can hang a stocking from her foot. We posed her with a tiny holly basket under one arm. Bend the other hand inward, to give her a little character.

9. Slip the shirt down over the top of the beanbag. Untie the neck knot of the head. Place the elf's head on top of this assembly, inserting the neck edges of the shirt and beanbag up into the neck opening of the head. Turn under a hem all the way around the neck edge of the head, and whipstitch around the neck several times to secure the head to the body.

10. Wrap the collar around the elf's neck, overlapping and glueing the ends at the center back. Glue a red sequin to the right side of the collar at each point (optional).

Finishing

1. Wrap the belt around the elf's waist, overlapping and glueing the ends together at the center front.

2. Glue the buckle to the front of the belt.

3. We positioned one of the male elves so that he will sit upright, and you can hang a stocking from one foot. To do this, bend his right leg up and across his left leg, so that his right foot will touch his left hand. Wrap the end of the hand around the foot, and glue them together securely. The left leg will hang down over the edge of the mantel, to hold the stocking as shown in **Figure N**.

THE FEMALE ELF

The female elf is made in basically the same manner as the male elf, but she has long braids and wears a skirt.

Materials

One leg of nurse's white pantyhose
A small amount of polyester fiberfill
Heavy-duty white thread and a long sharp needle
Two black-headed straight pins, for the eyes
Small scrap of black felt
10 x 20-inch square of white polyester knit fabric, for the wings
5 foot length of ⅛-inch-diameter white nylon cord
6-inch length of ¼-inch-diameter metal rod or wooden dowel rod (We used the handle of a small plastic paintbrush.)
4½-inch length of 4 x 4 pine (You will have to drill a socket into one end to accommodate the rod.)
Wire clothes hanger, or florist's wire (One of the lightweight white hangers has the right amount of bendability. If you use florist's wire, you might need to double the strand for sufficient strength.)
White glue or hot-melt glue and a glue gun
Stain or varnish

Making the Body

1. A scale drawing of the Body piece is given in **Figure A**. Enlarge the drawing to make a full-size pattern.
2. Cut a 10-inch section from the pantyhose leg. Place the full-size Body pattern on the double thickness of hose, positioning the straight pattern edge on a fold, and cut out the Body.
3. Stitch the two layers of the body together, leaving the tail open to allow for turning and stuffing (**Figure C**).
4. Turn the body right side out, so the seam is on the inside. Stuff the body with fiberfill, working through the opening in the tail. Stuff the beak very lightly. Refer to **Figure D** to shape the body. Do not stuff the tail. As you stuff, keep the sewn seam along the bottom center of the body.

Egret

You won't re-gret making this e-gret. In fact, you might even break into song, "E-grets, I've had a few..." and when you finish creating this snowy-white bird you can add, "I did it my-y-y way-y-y!"

1 square = 1 inch

Figure A

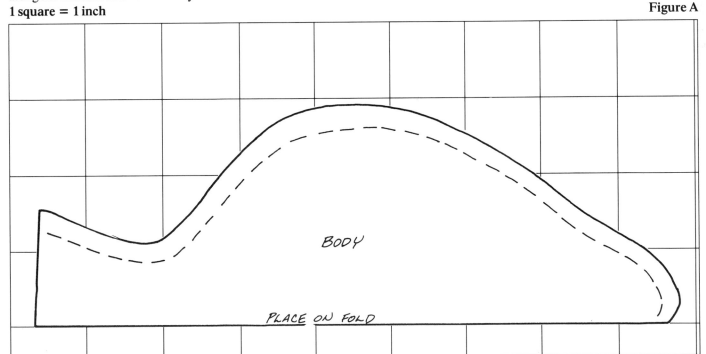

BODY

PLACE ON FOLD

Figure B

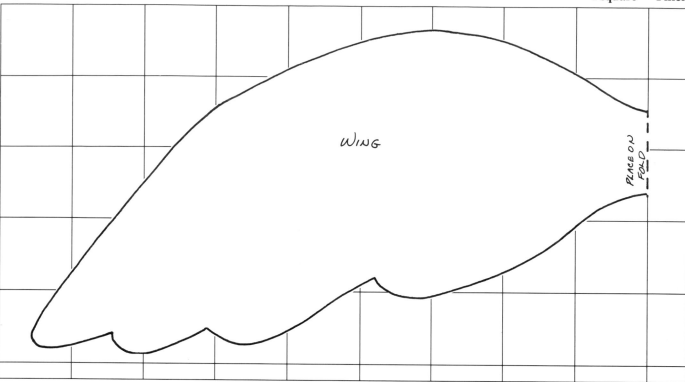

WING

PLACE ON FOLD

Figure C

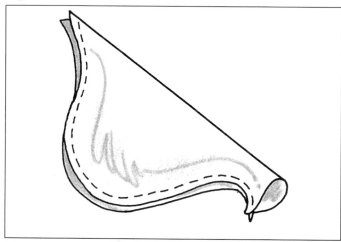

Figure D

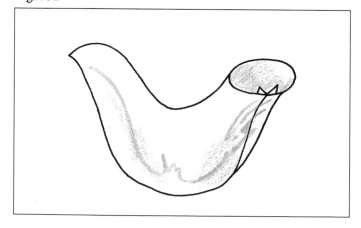

5. When the body is sufficiently stuffed, flatten the tail across the back and sew across the stitching line to close the opening (**Figure E**).

Making the Tail

1. The tail is left unstuffed, but the pantyhose is sculpted to create tail feathers.

2. Turn the raw edge of the tail to the inside and whipstitch the edges together.

3. To sculpt the tail, follow the entry and exit points illustrated in **Figure F**. Use a long sharp needle and heavy-duty white thread.

    a. Enter the needle on the underside of the tail and exit at point 1.

    b. Stitch along the broken line between 1 and 2. Exit at 2.

    c. Take a small stitch at 2 to lock the thread securely at point 2.

    d. Reenter at 2 and exit at 3.

    e. Take a small stitch at point 3 to secure the thread.

    f. Stitch along the broken line between 3 and 4, exiting at point 4.

    g. Reenter at 4 and exit at 5.

    h. Stitch along the broken line between 5 and 6. Exit at 6. Take a small stitch at point 6 to lock the thread securely.

    i. Lock the stitch and cut the thread.

Making the Wings

1. A scale drawing of the Wing is provided in **Figure B**. Enlarge the drawing to make a full-size pattern.

2. Fold the 10 x 20-inch rectangle of white double-knit fabric

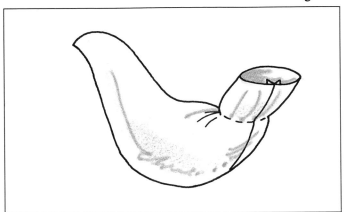

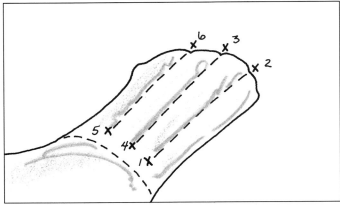

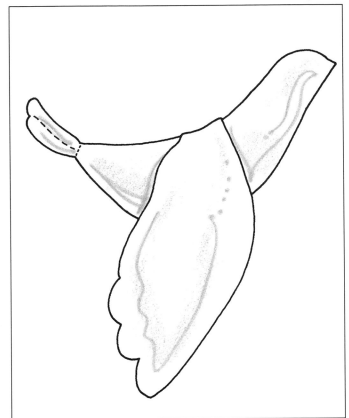

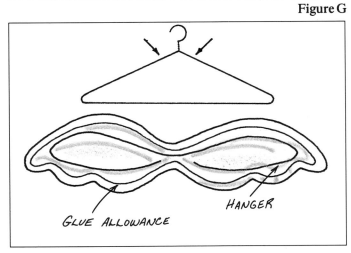

GLUE ALLOWANCE   HANGER

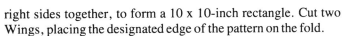

Figure I

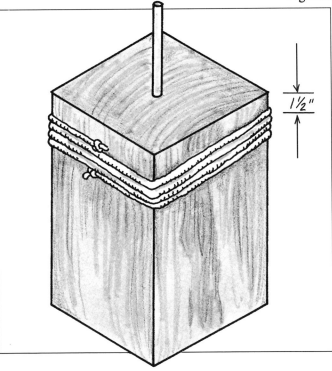

1½"

right sides together, to form a 10 x 10-inch rectangle. Cut two Wings, placing the designated edge of the pattern on the fold.

3. Place one Wing right side down on a flat surface.

4. If you use the wire clothes hanger, cut off the curved end, as shown in **Figure G**.

5. Bend and shape the wire following the contours of the Wing, allowing a ½-inch-wide glue allowance all around the outside edge. Place the shaped wire on top of the Wing, as shown in **Figure G**.

6. Run a bead of glue around the outer edge of the Wing. Place the second Wing right side up on top of the first, matching

the edges and sandwiching the wire between the layers. Let the glue dry.

7. Position the wings across the Egret's back and glue or tack them in place, as shown in **Figure H**.

Figure J

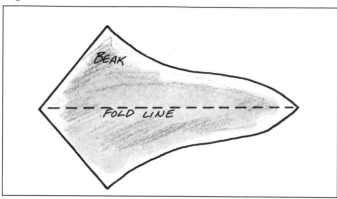

BEAK

FOLD LINE

Figure K

Figure L

Making the Base

1. Drill a shallow socket into one end of the 4 x 4. Glue one end of the rod into the socket.

2. Finish the wooden base, using stain or varnish.

3. Tie a knot in one end of the 5-foot length of white nylon cord. Glue the tied end to the base approximately 1½ inches from the top. Wrap the cord around the base four times, ending on the same side as the starting point. Tie a knot in the end of the cord, and cut off the excess. Glue the knotted end to the base. **Figure I** shows the completed base.

Finishing

1. Cut one Beak from the scrap of black felt, using the full-size pattern provided in **Figure J**. Fold the beak in half along the fold line. Glue the long lower edges together so that it forms a cone. Slip the felt beak over the pantyhose beak, and glue the completed beak to the Egret, as shown in **Figure K**.

2. Temporarily position the bird on top of the rod to determine the best arrangement. It should be as balanced as possible. Spread glue over the end of the rod, and insert it into the bottom of the bird.

3. Glue two black-headed straight pins into the head for the eyes (**Figure L**).

Materials

One leg from a pair of regular-weave flesh-tone pantyhose
½ yard of 36-inch-wide medium-weight cotton or cotton blend fabric for the body (We used a red-and-beige striped fabric.)
9 x 18-inch piece of bandanna fabric in red or another color that coordinates with the body fabric
16 x 24-inch piece of vinyl fabric or felt in a color that coordinates with the body fabric, for the hat
Small scraps of black felt
Two ½-inch-diameter black buttons for the eyes
4½ yards of black rug yarn for the hair
¾ yard of 1-inch-wide ribbon for the hatband (We used white.)
Regular sewing thread to match the fabrics
Heavy-duty flesh-tone thread and a long sharp needle
A toy sheriff's badge (Or, you can make one from aluminum foil glued to a cardboard backing.)
White glue or hot-melt glue and a glue gun
A bag of polyester fiberfill

Adjusting the Body Pattern

In order for Clem to do his job well, the Body pattern should be altered to fit a specific pair of boots. This is quite easy to do.

1. A scale drawing of the Body pattern is provided in **Figure A**. Enlarge the drawing to make a full-size pattern. If you plan to make a bootsaver for several different pairs of boots, keep this full-size pattern as an original, and trace the pattern before making any alterations on the tracing.

2. To check for fit, first measure the inside diameter of your boot, at the ankle and at the top. Measure the inside depth of the boot as well, from the heel to the top. Now measure the traced full-size Body pattern. If the ankle measurement of your boot is longer or shorter than the "ankle line" indicated on the pattern, make a note of the difference on the pattern. Do the same for the "top line" indicated on the pattern. Now measure the vertical distance between the "top line" and the lower seam line on the pattern. If it is different than the inside depth measurement of your boot, make a note of the difference.

3. To adjust the pattern, start with the vertical measurement. If your boot is taller or shorter than the depth of the pattern, cut across the pattern between the "ankle line" and the "top line." Then, either overlap the two sections or spread them apart to make the depth adjustment. If you spread them apart, tape the two sections to a separate piece of paper, using a ruler to align the edges.

4. The ankle and top measurements should be adjusted so that the bootsaver will fit tightly inside your boots, to keep them straight. This being the case, the widthwise measurements of the pattern should be slightly longer than those taken inside your boot. If you need to adjust them, place a piece of tracing or pattern paper on top of the pattern, and mark the adjusted seam lines at the ends of the "ankle line" and at the ends of the "top line." Place a ruler along the adjusted markings and connect the ankle and top markings on each side with a dotted line, to indicate the new seam line. Draw a straight line ½ inch outside each

Bootsaver Clem Clodhopper

Howdy pardner! The sheriff's here to uphold law and order…and the shape of your boots. They will stand at attention as long as Clem's on duty, saving that expensive leather from the wear and tear of a bendable life. Clem's size can be adjusted to fit any boot size.

new dotted line, to indicate the new cutting lines. Retrace all other cutting lines from the original pattern, along the edges that have not been adjusted. You should now have a new pattern that will fit your boots perfectly.

Cutting the Pieces

1. Scale drawings for the Bandanna, Hat Crown, and Hat Brim are provided in **Figure A**. Enlarge the drawings to make full-size patterns. (No alterations will be necessary.) Trace the full-size patterns for the Eyebrow and Mustache provided in **Figure B**.

2. Cut two Body pieces from cotton fabric, using the altered pattern you made.

3. Cut one Bandanna from bandanna fabric.

4. Cut two Hat Crowns and one Hat Brim from vinyl or felt.

5. Cut two Eyebrows and one Mustache from black felt.

Figure A

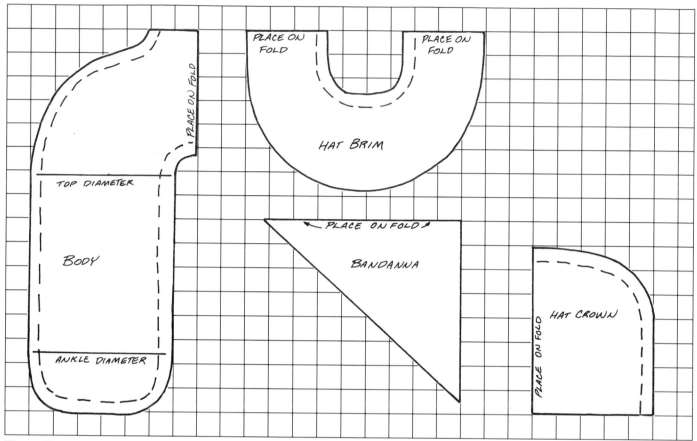

Figure B

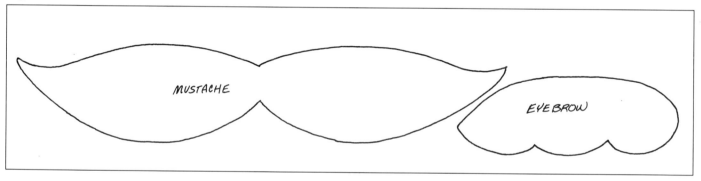

Making the Body

Note: All seams are ½ inch wide unless otherwise specified in the instructions.

1. Unfold the two Body pieces (they should be horseshoe-shaped), and pin them right sides together. Stitch the seam all the way along the long contoured edge, as shown in **Figure C**, leaving the straight neck edge open. Clip the curves and turn the body right side out. Press the seam allowance to the inside around the open neck edge.

2. Stuff the body tightly with fiberfill.

Making the Head

1. To form the head, tie a knot below the panty line of the leg of regular pantyhose. Cut the leg from the panty about 1 inch above the knot, and cut across the hose about 10 inches below the knot. Turn the hose so that the knot is on the inside, and stuff with fiberfill until the head is approximately 5½ inches in diameter. Tie the hose in a knot at the neck, and trim the excess hose below the knot.

2. Follow the entry and exit points illustrated in **Figure D** to soft-sculpt the facial features.

    a. Enter at 1, push the needle through the center of the head, and exit at 2. To form the nose, sew a circle of basting stitches about 2 inches in diameter, and exit at point 3.

    b. Use the tip of the needle to gently lift the fiberfill within the circle. Pull the thread until a round nose appears, lock the stitch, and exit at 2.

    c. To form the nostrils, reenter at 2 and exit at 4.

Figure C

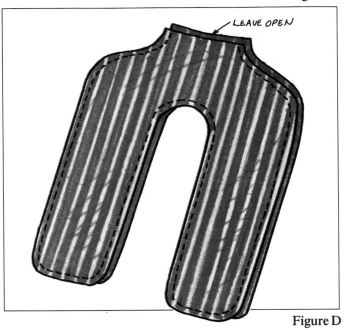

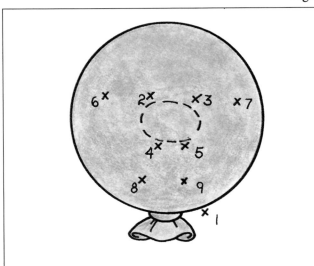

d. Reenter about ¼ inch above 4 and exit at 3.

e. Reenter at 3 and exit at 5.

f. Reenter about ¼ inch above 5 and exit at 2. Pull the thread until the nostrils appear and lock the stitch, exiting at 2.

g. To form the eye lines, pull the thread across the surface, enter at 6, and exit at 3.

h. Pull the thread across the surface, enter at 7, and exit at 2. Gently pull the thread to form the eye lines and lock the stitch, exiting at 2.

i. To form the mouth, reenter at 2 and exit at 8. Pull the thread across the surface, enter at 9, and exit at 2. Gently pull the thread until a smile forms. Lock the stitch and cut the thread.

3. Clem's face, with all the features in place, is shown in **Figure E**. Glue or whipstitch the Eyebrows and Mustache to the face as shown. Glue or stitch a black button over each eye line.

4. To make Clem's hair, cut the rug yarn into twenty 8-inch lengths. Stack them in a neat bunch and use a spare piece of yarn to tie them together at the center. Lay the yarn bunch across Clem's head, placing the tied center over the knot in the hose. Stitch the center of the yarn bunch to his head.

5. Insert the tied neck edge of Clem's head inside the neck opening in the body. Start at the center back and whipstitch around the neck several times to secure the head to the body.

Making the Bandanna and Hat

1. Unfold the Bandanna piece and press a very narrow hem to the wrong side of the fabric along each edge. Turn each of these edges under again, to form a double-turned hem. Stitch the hem.

Figure G

Figure H

Figure I

2. Wrap the bandanna around Clem's neck and tie the ends in a knot at one side.

3. Pin the two Hat Crown pieces right sides together. Stitch the seam along the long contoured edge, as shown in **Figure F**, leaving the straight lower edge open. Clip the curves and turn the crown right side out.

4. Fold or press the seam allowance toward the wrong side of the hat crown all the way around the lower raw edge, so that the folded seam allowance is at right angles to the sides of the crown (**Figure G**). Clip the seam allowance so that it lies flat.

5. Place the Brim piece right side up on a flat surface and spread a ½-inch-wide band of glue along the edge of the inner oval opening. Place the crown on top, aligning the folded, clipped edge with the edge of the oval opening in the brim. Press the edges together tightly. If you are using white glue instead of hot-melt, we suggest that you use straight pins or clothespins to hold the edges together until the glue dries.

6. Wrap the length of ribbon around the bottom of the hat crown, overlapping the ends at one end of the center crown seam. Glue the ribbon hatband in place and cut off the excess at each end.

7. Roll up the sides of the brim, as shown in **Figure H**, and glue the edges to the crown to hold them in place. Crease the top of the crown inward along the seam.

8. Spread Clem's hair out to the sides and place his hat on top. Adjust it to your satisfaction, and glue or tack the hat to his head (**Figure I**).

9. Pin Clem's sheriff badge to his shoulder, and he's ready to protect your boots.

Materials

For the ballerina:

One leg of regular flesh-tone pantyhose

6½-inch length of 45-inch-wide unbleached muslin

8 x 8-inch piece of black felt

2 yards of 4-inch-wide gathered white eyelet trim

23-inch length of ⅜-inch-wide pink satin ribbon

24 yards of yarn for the hair (We used dark brown.)

1¼ yards of ½-inch-wide black seam tape, grosgrain, or satin ribbon for the shoe ties

3 x 36-inch piece of nylon net

Three pink pinwheel beads

Heavy-duty flesh-tone thread; a long sharp needle; and thread to match the fabric

For the clown:

One leg of white pantyhose

14 x 45-inch rectangle of fabric for the legs and hat (We used a heavy cotton duck fabric in a multi-colored stripe.)

Four pieces of red felt, each 5 x 9 inches; and one piece of red felt, 2 x 2 inches

Two 10-inch squares of yellow flannel

½ skein of red rug yarn for the hair

Several long craft pipe cleaners of any color

Nine 1-inch-diameter red pompoms for the hat and ankles

Two yards of double-fold bias tape in a color that coordinates with the clown's leg fabric

Heavy-duty white thread; a long sharp needle; and thread to match the fabrics

You will also need:

A bag of polyester fiberfill

Cosmetic cheek blusher

Black and red felt-tip pens or fabric marking pens

White glue or hot-melt glue and a glue gun

THE BALLERINA

The ballerina's legs form the actual draft stopper. Her head is made separately, and is then stitched to the legs. An eyelet collar covers the neck seam. To fit the draft stopper to a particular door or window, measure the length of the area you wish to cover, and alter the length of the muslin rectangle to fit. It should still be 6½ inches wide, and about 1 inch longer than the area to be covered.

Making the Legs

Note: All seams are ½ inch wide unless otherwise specified in the instructions.

1. Fold the muslin rectangle in half lengthwise with right sides together. Stitch a straight seam along the long edge, leaving a 6-inch opening at the center, and stitch a curved seam across each short end, as shown in **Figure A**. Trim the excess seam allowances along the curved ends. Clip the curves.

2. Turn the tube right side out, bringing the ends through the opening. Stuff the tube with fiberfill, using the blunt end of a pencil or long knitting needle to push the fiberfill into the ends.

Clown & Ballerina Draft Stoppers

Do you use rolled-up towels to stop cold winter winds that whistle under your doors? Now you can stitch up one of our adorable draft stoppers to handle the task efficiently and beautifully. The ballerina will be perfect for a little girl's room, and the clown will fit anywhere there are cold people who need a warm chuckle.

Press the seam allowances to the inside along the edges of the opening, and whipstitch the opening edges together.

3. A scale drawing for the Ballet Shoe is provided in **Figure B**. Enlarge the drawing to make a full-size pattern, and cut four Ballet Shoe pieces from the black felt.

4. Place two Ballet Shoe pieces together and stitch the seam all the way along the long curved edge. Leave the straight, angled edge open and unstitched (**Figure C**). Trim the seam allowances to ¼ inch, clip the curve, and turn the shoe right side out.

5. Cut two 10-inch lengths of black seam binding, grosgrain, or satin ribbon. Stitch one length to the wrong side of the fabric on each side of the shoe, where indicated in **Figure C**.

6. Repeat the procedures in steps 4 and 5 to make the second shoe, using the two remaining Ballet Shoe pieces and two additional lengths of seam tape or ribbon.

7. Slip one of the shoes over one end of the leg tube, and wrap

Figure A

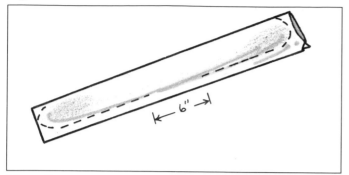

Figure B

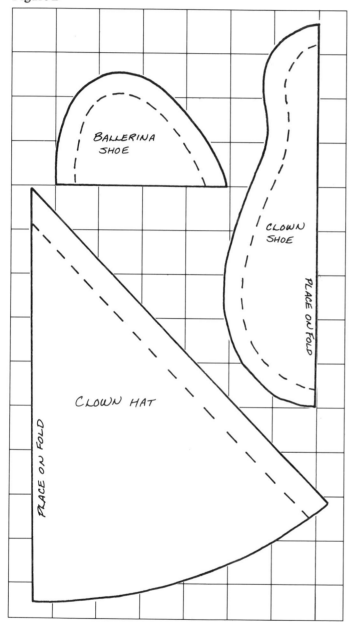

BALLERINA SHOE

CLOWN SHOE

PLACE ON FOLD

CLOWN HAT

PLACE ON FOLD

the two ribbons around the leg in a criss-cross pattern. Tie the ends in a bow or knot. Install the remaining shoe on the other foot, in the same manner.

Figure C

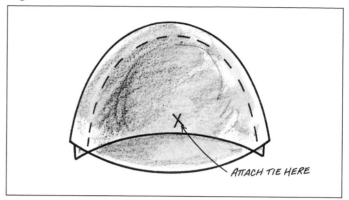

ATTACH TIE HERE

Figure D

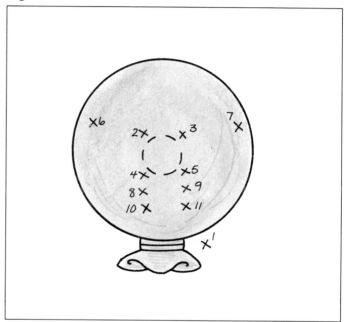

Making the Head

1. Tie a knot in one leg of regular-weave pantyhose near the panty line. Cut across the hose about 1 inch above the knot, and about 10 inches below the knot. Turn the hose so the knot is on the inside, and stuff with fiberfill until the head is approximately 5 inches in diameter. Tie the hose in a knot at the neck and trim off the excess hose below the knot.

2. Follow the entry and exit points illustrated in **Figure D** to sculpt the facial features, using a long sharp needle and heavy-duty flesh-tone thread.

    a. Enter at 1, push the needle through the center of the head, and exit at 2. To form the nose, sew a circle of basting stitches about the size of a silver dollar, and exit at 3.

    b. Use the tip of the needle carefully to lift fiberfill within the circle, and gently pull the thread until a little round nose appears. Lock the stitch, reenter at 3, and exit at point 2.

    c. To form the nostrils, reenter at 2 and exit at 4.

    d. Reenter ¼ inch above 4 and exit at 3.

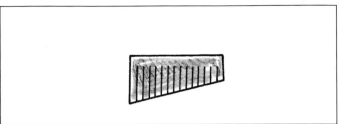

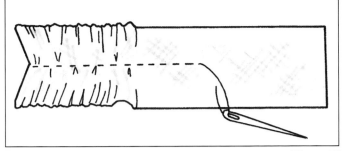

3. The ballerina's eyelashes are cut from black felt. A full-size pattern is provided in **Figure E**. Cut two Eyelashes, and glue them to the eye lines.

4. Place the head at the center of the leg tube, so that the leg seam runs along the bottom. Whipstitch around the head several times to secure it to the tube; the collar will cover the stitches.

5. To make the ballerina's hair, cut twenty-four strands of yarn, each 1 yard long. Gather the strands into an even pile and wrap a piece of thread around the center of the strands. Stitch the center to the top of the ballerina's head, as shown in **Figure F**. At each side, about where the bottom of the ear would be if she had one, stitch the yarn to the head as shown. Braid the yarn below these stitches on each side, and secure by tying a short length of yarn around each braid near the end. We rolled up each braid into a knot, and secured the knotted braid with a few stitches.

6. Run a line of basting stitches along the center length of the nylon net rectangle, as shown in **Figure G**. Gather the net tightly and lock the stitch, but do not cut the thread. Continue working with the same thread to tack the gathered net bow to the top center of the head, over the hair. Tack the pinwheel beads to the center of the net bow.

7. To finish the ballerina's face, draw eyebrows, using the black marker or pen. Use the red marker to draw an upper lip above the mouth stitches, and a lower lip between the two mouth stitches, as shown in **Figure H**. Brush cosmetic blusher across the cheeks.

e. Reenter at 3 and exit at 5.

f. Reenter about ¼ inch above 5 and exit at 2. Pull the thread and lock the stitch at point 2.

g. To form the eye lines, pull the thread across the surface, enter at 6, and exit at 3.

h. Pull the thread across the surface, enter at 7, and exit at 2. Pull the thread gently to form the eyes lines. Lock the stitch at point 2.

i. To form the mouth, reenter at 2 and exit at 8.

j. Pull the thread across the surface, enter at 9, and exit at 2. Pull gently to form the mouth line and lock the stitch at 2.

k. To form the lower lip, reenter at 2 and exit at 10. Pull the thread across the surface, enter at 11, and exit at 2. Pull gently to form the lower lip, and lock the stitch at point 2.

l. Reenter at point 2 and exit at 1. Lock the stitch and cut the thread.

Figure I

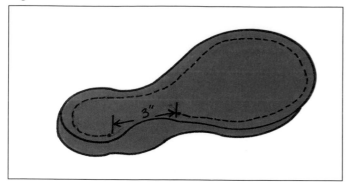

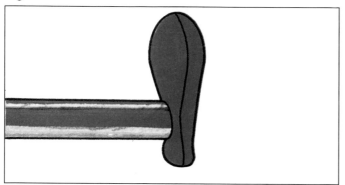

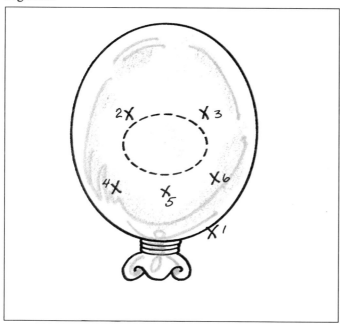

Figure L

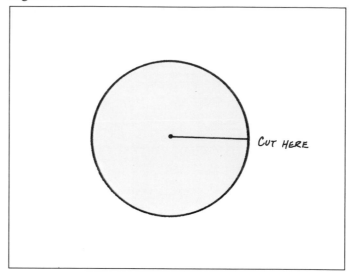

CUT HERE

Making the Collar

1. Run a line of long basting stitches close to the bound edge of the gathered eyelet trim. Pull up the basting stitches to gather the trim even more, and place it around the ballerina's neck. Adjust the gathers so the ends just overlap at the back, and tack the collar to the neck.

2. Wrap the length of pink satin ribbon around the ballerina's neck and tie it in a bow at the front.

THE CLOWN

The clown draft stopper consists of a leg tube with a shoe on each end. A ruffled flannel collar covers the neck seam, and a conical clown's hat perches on top of a red rug yarn wig.

Making the Legs

1. Measure the width of the door or window along which you plan to use the clown. Cut a rectangle from the fabric you have chosen for the clown, 6½ inches wide and 1 inch *shorter* than the measured width, to allow for his big feet.

2. Fold the rectangle in half lengthwise, placing right sides together, and stitch the seam along the long edge only. Do not stitch across the ends.

3. Turn the tube right side out, press the seam allowance to the inside around each open end, and stuff the tube tightly with fiberfill.

4. A scale drawing for the Clown Shoe is provided in **Figure B**. Enlarge the drawing to make a full-size pattern.

5. Fold one of the red felt rectangles in half lengthwise and cut one Clown Shoe piece, placing the designated edge of the pattern along the fold. Cut three additional Clown Shoe pieces, using the three remaining red felt rectangles.

6. Place two Clown Shoe pieces together and stitch the seam all the way around the outer edge, leaving a 3-inch opening on one side (**Figure I**). Clip the curves, turn the shoe right side out, and press the seam allowances to the inside along the opening edges. Stuff the shoe firmly with fiberfill and whipstitch the opening edges together.

7. Repeat the procedures in step 6 to make a second shoe, using the remaining two Clown Shoe pieces.

8. Place the leg tube on a flat surface so that the seam is on the bottom. Place one shoe against one open end of the leg tube with the toe end pointing upward, and whipstitch it securely in place (**Figure J**). Glue four small red pompoms around the ankle to cover the seam.

9. Repeat the procedures in step 8 to attach the remaining shoe to the opposite end of the leg tube, making sure that both feet point in the same direction.

MORE GREAT PANTYHOSE CRAFTS

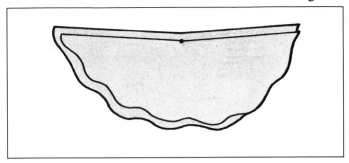

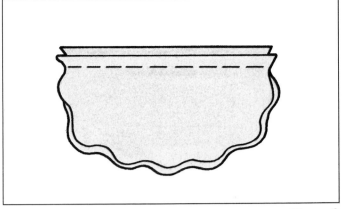

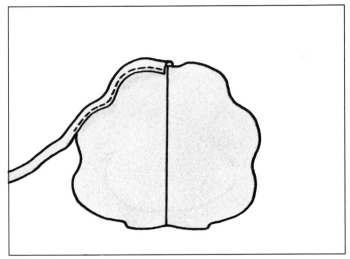

Making the Head

1. Tie a knot in the white pantyhose near the panty line. Cut off the leg about 1 inch above the knot, and about 10 inches below the knot. Turn the hose so the knot is on the inside. Stuff with fiberfill until the head is about 5 inches in diameter. Tie the hose in a knot at the neck and trim the excess hose below the knot.

2. Follow the entry and exit points illustrated in **Figure K** as you sculpt the facial features, using a long sharp needle and heavy-duty thread.

    a. Enter at 1, push the needle through the center of the head, and exit at 2. To form the nose, sew a circle of basting stitches 2 inches in diameter, and exit at 3.

    b. Use the tip of the needle carefully to lift fiberfill within the circle, and pull the thread gently until the nose appears. Lock the stitch, reenter at 3, and exit at 2.

    c. To form the mouth, reenter at 2 and exit at 4.

    d. Pull the thread across the surface, enter at 5, and exit at 6. Pull the thread across the surface, enter at 5, and exit at 2. Pull the thread until a smile appears. Lock the stitch and cut the thread.

3. Use the black marker or pen to draw the lip line. Draw his big nose, using the red marker. In addition, draw two red cheek circles, and when the ink is dry brush cheek blusher across the clown's cheeks. The eye area will be hidden by hair, so there's no need to draw or sculpt eyes.

4. A scale drawing for the Hat is provided in **Figure B**. Enlarge the drawing to make a full-size pattern.

5. Cut one Hat piece from the same fabric you used for the leg tube. Note that the fabric should be doubled, and the designated edge of the pattern placed on the fold.

6. Fold the Hat piece along the "place on fold" line, with right sides together, and stitch the seam along the long straight edge only. Turn the hat right side out and press the seam allowance to the inside around the circular lower edge. Stitch a red pompom to the point of the hat.

7. To make the clown's hair, wrap the half skein of rug yarn into a continuous loop about 8 inches in diameter. Gather and tie the loop at the center so that it forms a figure eight. Cut the ends of the loops on each side. Whipstitch the tied center of the yarn to the top of the clown's head at the pantyhose knot, and spread the hair out around the top of the head. Trim the ends if the hair is too long.

8. Glue or whipstitch the hat to the clown's hair and head. Do not attach the head to the leg tube just yet.

Making the Collar

1. Cut a 10-inch-diameter circle from each of the squares of yellow flannel. Cut along the radius of each circle, from the outer edge straight in to the center of the circle (**Figure L**).

2. Place the two flannel circles together, aligning the radius cuts. Grasp the corners formed by the radius cuts and pull them outward until the two edges of each cut form a straight line (**Figure M**). Stitch a seam through both flannel layers along the radius cut edge, as shown in **Figure N**. Open out the two layers of flannel, and press the seam open.

3. Use the double-fold bias tape to encase the entire outer raw edge of the collar, as shown in **Figure O**. Leave the ends open.

4. Twist the pipe cleaners together end to end so you have one long piece, and thread it through the casing around the outer edge of the collar. Cut off any excess pipe cleaner that extends beyond the ends of the casing, and stitch across the ends so the pipe cleaner can't work its way out. Bend the pipe cleaner inside the casing so the collar has a ruffled look.

5. Place the leg tube on a flat surface, with the toes pointing upward. Place the collar on top, at the center of the tube. Place the clown's head on top of the collar, at the center. Whipstitch around the neck, through the collar, and into the leg tube, to secure the assembly.

Roller Derby Queenie

Roller-skating is high on the list of fun things to do these days, and who better to illustrate the state of the art than Queenie. She's a pert little doll, complete with roller skates, who will roll away with your heart. Queenie stands 18 inches tall.

Materials

One regular-weave flesh-tone stocking or one leg from a pair of pantyhose
¾ yard of flesh-tone fleece fabric for the body
½ yard of deep purple velour for the skating suit
¾ yard of deep pink velour for the skirt and sleeves
½ yard of lightweight white cotton fabric for the boots and pant lining pieces.
One skein of yellow mohair yarn for the hair and eyelashes
2½ yards of ⅛-inch-wide hot pink ribbon for the ponytail, boot, and dress ties
12-inch length of ⅛-inch-wide elastic
A bag of polyester fiberfill
Sewing thread to match the fabrics and yarn; heavy-duty flesh-tone thread; and a long sharp needle
White glue or hot-melt glue and a glue gun
Cosmetic cheek blusher
12-inch length of ³⁄₁₆-inch-diameter wooden dowel rod for the skate axles

Eight wooden wheels, each 1 inch in diameter and about ¼ inch thick, for the skate boots (You can find these at many hobby shops. The wheels should have axle holes that are ³⁄₁₆ inch in diameter.)

Cutting the Pieces

1. Scale drawings for the Skirt, Torso/Leg, Pants, Bodice, Sleeve, Arm, Boot Front, Boot Sole, and Boot Heel are provided in **Figure A**. Enlarge the drawings to make full-size patterns, and transfer all placement markings to the patterns. Note that the Torso/Leg pattern shows a slight difference in cutting lines for the Front Torso/Leg piece than the Back Torso/Leg piece. Note also that the Bodice pattern should be placed on a fold of doubled fabric when you cut the Bodice Front, but it should be used to cut two separate pieces for the Bodice Backs.

2. Cut the pieces listed here from flesh-colored fleece.
Arm – cut four
Back Torso/Leg – cut one
Front Torso/Leg – cut one

3. Cut the pieces listed here from deep purple velour.
Bodice Front – cut one
Bodice Back – cut two
Pants – cut two

4. Cut the pieces listed in this step from pink velour. (See Tips & Techniques, if necessary, for instructions on how to cut bias strips.)
Skirt Binding Strip – cut one, 1¾ x 28 inches (bias)
Neck Binding Strip – cut one, 1¾ x 14 inches (bias)
Sleeves – cut two
Skirt – cut three

5. Cut the pieces listed in this step from the white fabric.
Pants – cut two
Boot Front – cut two
Boot Heel – cut two
Boot Sole – cut two

Making the Head

1. Tie a knot just below the panty line in one leg of panythose. Cut across the hose about 1 inch above the knot, and again about 10 inches below the knot. Turn the hose so the knot is on the inside, and stuff with fiberfill until the head is approximately 5½ inches in diameter. Tie the hose in a knot at the neck and trim the excess hose below the knot.

2. Follow the entry and exit points illustrated in **Figure B** to sculpt the facial features.
   a. Enter at 1, guide the needle through the head, and exit at 2. To form the nose, sew a circle of basting stitches about the size of a silver dollar, and exit at 3.
   b. Use the tip of the needle to very carefully lift the fiberfill within the circle. Gently pull the thread until a little round nose appears. Lock the stitch and exit at 2.
   c. To form the nostrils, reenter at 2 and exit at 4.
   d. Reenter ¼ inch above 4 and exit at 3.

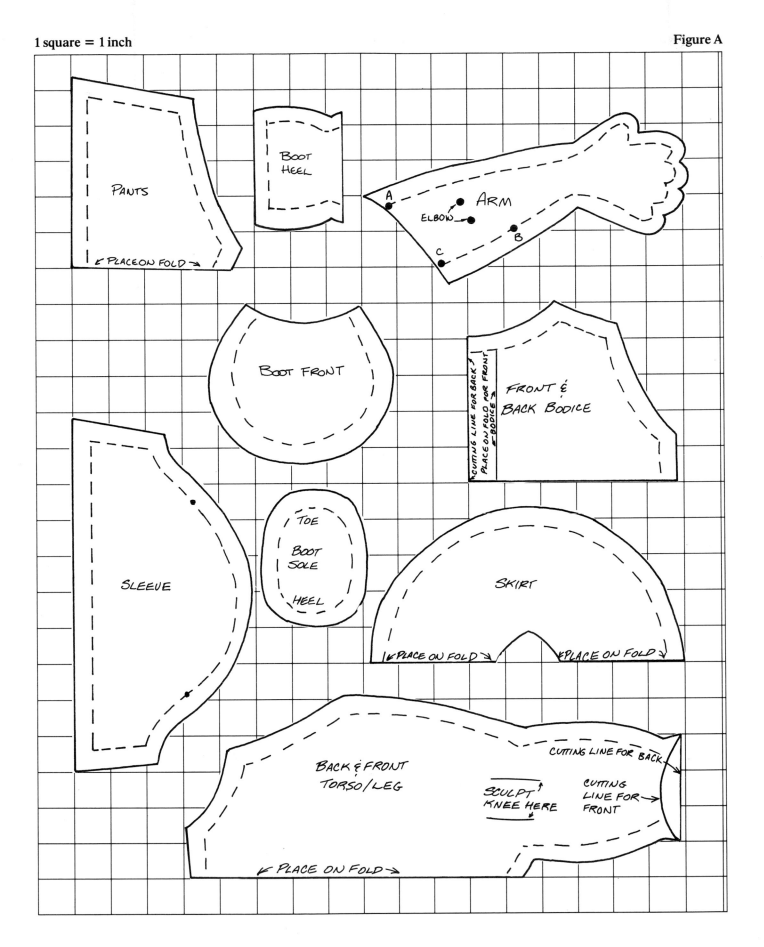

Figure B

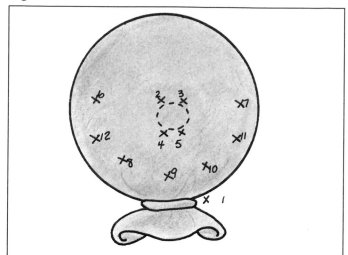

Figure C

Figure D

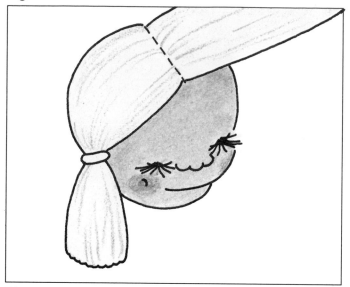

Figure E

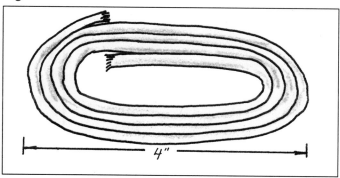

e. Reenter at 3 and exit at 5.

f. Reenter about ¼ inch above 5 and exit at 2. Pull the thread and lock the stitch at 2.

g. To form the eye lines, pull the thread across the surface, enter at 6, and exit at 3.

h. Pull the thread across the surface, enter at 7, and exit at 2. Pull the thread gently to form the eye lines and lock the stitch at 2.

i. To form the mouth, reenter at 2 and exit at 8.

j. Pull the thread across the surface, enter at 9, and exit at 10. Pull the thread across the surface, enter at 9, and exit at 2. Gently pull the thread until a smile appears, and lock the stitch at 2.

k. To form a dimple, reenter at 2 and exit at 11. Reenter at 11 and exit at 2. Pull the thread until a dimple appears, and lock the stitch at 2.

l. To form the second dimple, reenter at 2 and exit at 12. Reenter at 12 and exit at 2. Pull the thread until the second dimple appears, lock the stitch, and cut the thread.

3. Brush a little powdered cheek blusher across Queenie's nose and across each cheek.

4. We made Queenie's eyelashes of mohair yarn. For one eye, cut six or seven lengths of yarn, each about 1¼ inches long. Gather the lengths together in an even bunch and stitch the center of the bunch to Queenie's face, at the center of one eye line (**Figure C**). Fluff the ends of the yarn. Repeat these procedures to cut and attach eyelashes to the other eye line.

5. To make Queenie's hair, cut the remaining yarn into 20-inch lengths. Lay aside two of the strands for the time being. Take six or eight of the strands and stack them in an even bunch. Place this bunch across Queenie's head and stitch the center of the bunch to the top center of the head about 1½ inches in front of the pantyhose knot (**Figure D**). Take a second six- or eight-strand bunch and stitch it to the head in the same manner, just behind the first bunch. Continue stitching bunches of yarn to the head in this manner, working backward along the "center part" until you reach a point approximately 2½ inches behind the knot, on the back of the head.

6. To form the ponytail on one side of the head, spread the yarn evenly across the head on one side of the center part, and gather it together at about mouth level. Stitch the gathered yarn to the head at that point, and spot-glue the hair to the head above the gathered point to keep it in place. Cut an 18-inch length of narrow ribbon, wrap it around the ponytail so that it covers the stitches, and tie it in a bow at the front. Form a ponytail on the opposite side of the head in the same manner.

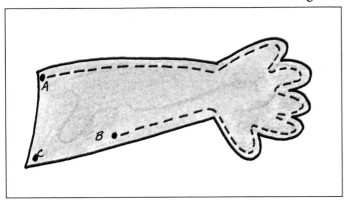

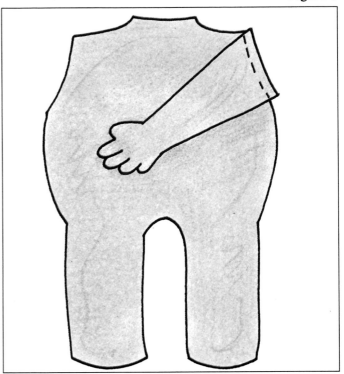

7. To form Queenie's bangs, take the two remaining strands of yarn that you set aside earlier and wrap them into a continuous loop, about 4 inches wide (**Figure E**). Gather the yarn loop at the center and stitch it to Queenie's face over the front hair strands, at the center part. Fluff the bangs, and Queenie's head is complete.

Making the Body

Note: Seams are ½ inch wide unless otherwise specified in the instructions.

1. To make one arm, pin two Arm pieces right sides together and stitch the seam along the long contoured edge, beginning at point A and ending at point B, as shown in **Figure F**. Leave the seam open between points B and C, and leave the shoulder edge open as shown. Clip the curves and corners and turn the arm right side out, using a pencil or other pointed object to turn the fingers. Press the seam allowances to the inside of the arm along the opening between points B and C.

2. Make a second arm in the same manner, using the two remaining Arm pieces.

3. Place the Back Torso/Leg piece right side up on a flat surface. Pin one assembled arm to the Back Torso piece, aligning the shoulder edge of the arm with the armhole edge of the Torso piece, and baste close to the edge, as shown in **Figure G**. (Be sure that the thumb is pointing upward.) Baste the other arm to the Back Torso piece in the same manner, aligning the shoulder edge with the armhole edge on the opposite side. Both thumbs should be pointing upward. Temporarily pin the lower ends of the arms out of the way of the torso seams.

4. Place the Front Torso piece right side down on top of this assembly. (The arms will be sandwiched between the two Torso pieces.) Stitch the torso seams, as shown in **Figure H**, leaving the neck and lower leg edges open. Clip the curves, turn the torso right side out, and press the seam allowance to the inside of the torso around the neck edge. Remove the pins that are holding the lower ends of the arms in place.

5. Place one Boot Front piece right side up on a flat surface. Place one Boot Heel piece right side down on top, aligning one side edge of the Heel piece with one side edge of the Front piece, as shown in **Figure I**. The upper edges of the two pieces should be even. Stitch the seam as shown, easing the Heel piece to fit, and press the seam open.

6. Now realign the two pieces, matching the opposite side

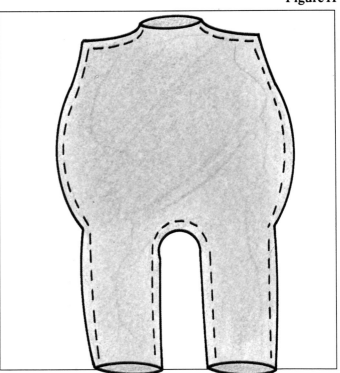

edges, and stitch the seam as you did before. Clip the corners and curves, but leave the partially assembled boot turned wrong side out.

7. The partial boot must be sewn to Queenie's leg before the sole is added. Turn the boot assembly upside down so that the larger opening for the sole is at the top, and the smaller opening

Figure I

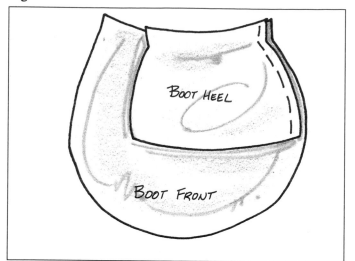

Figure L

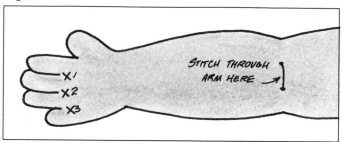

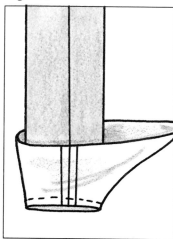
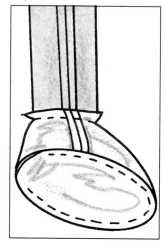

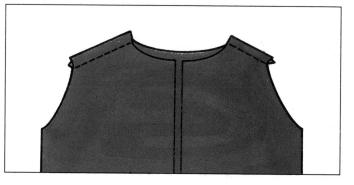

body through the neck and boot openings, and stuff each arm through the opening in the arm seam. Whipstitch the opening edges together along each arm and each boot, but leave the neck edge open.

Finishing the Body

1. To soft-sculpt the elbows, take a few stitches back and forth through each arm at the elbow points indicated on the Arm pattern, using a length of heavy-duty flesh-tone thread. One sculpted elbow is shown in **Figure L**.

2. Refer to **Figure L** as you sculpt the fingers on one hand, following the entry and exit points illustrated.

    a. To begin, insert the needle on the palm side of the hand at point 1, which is about ¾ inch inside the corner of the first finger. Push the needle straight through the hand and exit opposite point 1 on the back of the hand.

    b. Wrap the thread around the end of the hand, bringing it across the corner of the first finger, and enter at point 1 again.

    c. Push the needle underneath the surface, and exit at point 2 on the palm side of the hand. Pull the thread to tighten the first finger stitch.

    d. Reenter at 2, push the needle straight through the hand, and then exit directly opposite point 2 on the back side of the hand.

    e. Repeat the procedures in steps b, c, and d at point 2, and then at point 3, to form the remaining fingers. When you have finished, lock the stitch and cut the thread.

3. Repeat the procedures in step 2 to sculpt the fingers on the other hand.

4. To sculpt one knee, pinch up a small vertical ridge on the front of one leg. (The position of the ridge is indicated on the Torso pattern.) Stitch back and forth through the ridge a few times, lock the stitch, and cut the thread.

for the ankle is at the bottom. Slip the assembly up over the open end of one leg, and align the ankle edge of the boot with the ankle edge of the leg (**Figure J**). The leg should be right side out and the boot should be inside out, so that the fabrics are right sides together. Be sure that the boot assembly is turned so that the Boot Front piece is aligned with the front of the leg, and the Boot Heel piece is aligned with the back of the leg. Stitch the seam around the ankle, clip the curve, and turn the boot assembly downward.

8. Repeat the procedures in steps 5 through 7 to make the second partial boot assembly and stitch it to the other leg.

9. Turn the entire body assembly wrong side out. Pin one Sole piece inside the sole opening of one boot, placing right sides together. Make sure that the toe end of the sole is aligned along the Boot Front piece, and the heel end of the sole is aligned along the Boot Heel piece. Stitch the seam, as shown in **Figure K**, leaving a 2-inch opening along the heel portion of the seam. Clip the curves.

10. Attach the remaining Sole piece to the other boot assembly in the same manner.

11. Turn the body right side out and press the seam allowances to the inside along the opening in each boot. Stuff the

Figure N

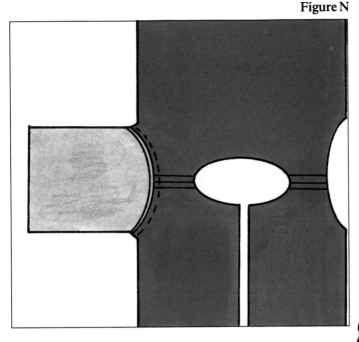

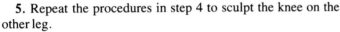

Figure O

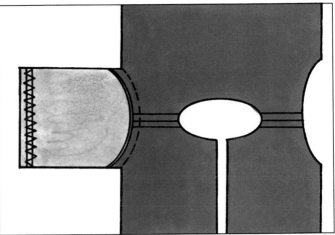

Figure P

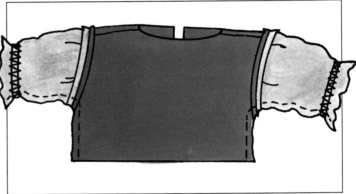

Figure Q

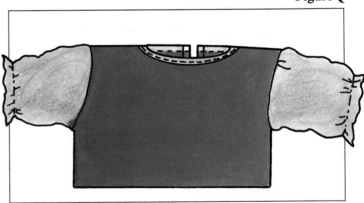

5. Repeat the procedures in step 4 to sculpt the knee on the other leg.

6. Place Queenie's head on top of her body, inserting the excess hose and the neck knot inside the neck opening of the body. Begin at the center back and whipstitch around the neck several times to secure it in place.

Making the Skating Suit Bodice

1. Place the velour Bodice Front piece right side up on a flat surface. Pin the two Bodice Back pieces right sides down on top and stitch the shoulder seam on each side, as shown in **Figure M**. Press the seams open.

2. Run a line of basting stitches along the curved upper edge of one Sleeve piece, just inside the seam line, between the dots indicated on the Sleeve pattern. Do not cut off the tails of thread.

3. Open out the bodice pieces and place the assembly right side up on a flat surface. Place the basted Sleeve piece right side down on top, aligning the curved upper edge with the armhole edge on one side of the bodice assembly. Pull up the basting threads to gather the edge of the Sleeve so that it fits the armhole edge. Adjust the gathers evenly and stitch the seam as shown in **Figure N**. Clip the curve and press the seam open.

4. Cut a 6-inch length of elastic. Place the elastic across the sleeve, on the wrong side of the fabric about 1¼ inches from the lower edge. Use a zigzag setting on your machine to stitch the elastic to the sleeve, stretching it as you go (**Figure O**) so that it extends from one side edge of the sleeve to the other.

5. Repeat the procedures in steps 2, 3, and 4 to attach the remaining Sleeve piece to the opposite armhole edge of the bodice assembly and to elasticise the sleeve end.

6. Fold the bodice-and-sleeve assembly right sides together and stitch the underarm and side seam on each side, as shown in **Figure P**. Press the seams open.

7. Turn and press a ¼-inch-wide hem to the wrong side of the fabric around the lower edge of each sleeve. Stitch the hems.

8. Turn and press a ½-inch-wide facing allowance to the wrong side of the fabric along the center back edge of each Bodice Back piece. Baste across the facing near the neck edge and near the lower edge to hold the facing in place.

9. Turn the bodice assembly right side out. To finish the neck edge, use the 14-inch Neck Binding Strip. To do this, first pin the Neck Binding Strip to the neck edge of the bodice, placing right sides together and aligning one long edge of the Binding Strip with the raw neck edge. The Strip should extend equally beyond each corner at the center back opening. Stitch the seam (**Figure Q**), clip the curves, and turn the Neck Binding Strip upward. Press the seam allowances toward the Strip.

Figure R

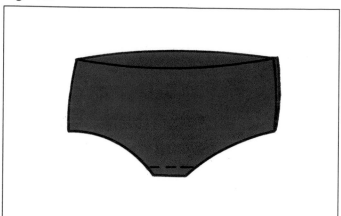

Figure S

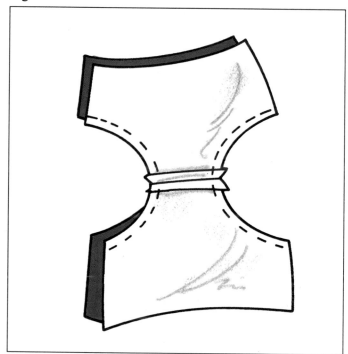

Figure T

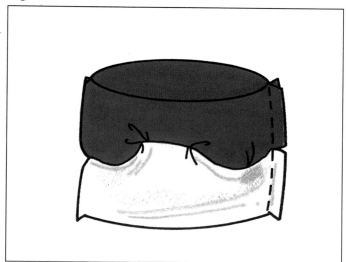

Figure U

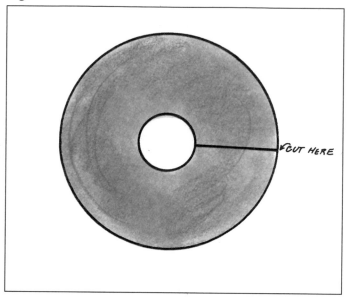

CUT HERE

10. Press a ½-inch-wide allowance to the wrong side of the Neck Binding Strip along the free long edge. Now fold the Strip in half lengthwise, placing wrong sides together, so that it encases the raw neck edge, and then whipstitch the pressed edge of the Strip to the wrong side of the bodice. Turn the ends of the Strip to the wrong side at the center back opening and tack them both in place.

11. Cut two 9-inch lengths of ribbon for the ties that will hold the suit together at the back neck edge. Fold one end of one ribbon, and stitch the folded end to the wrong side of the suit at one center back corner. Fold and stitch the remaining ribbon tie to the opposite corner in the same manner. Cut the free end of each ribbon tie at an angle.

Making the Suit Pants

1. Place the two velour Pants pieces right sides together and stitch the crotch seam only, as shown in **Figure R**. Clip the curve and press the seam open.

2. Repeat the procedures described in step 1, using the two Pants pieces that were cut from white fabric.

3. Open out the two halves of the velour pants assembly and place it right side up on a flat surface. Pin the white pants assembly right side down on top, and stitch the curved leg seam on each side, as shown in **Figure S**. Clip the curves, turn the assembly right sides out, and press the seams.

4. Fold the two halves of the white pants right sides together, so that the waist edges are aligned, and then align and pin the side edges together on each side. Fold and pin together the two halves of the velour pants in the same manner. Begin at one side of the waist edge of the velour pants, and stitch the side seam down to the leg seam, then continue to stitch the side seam of the white pants until you reach the waist edge (**Figure T**). Stitch the side seams on the opposite side of the assembly in the same manner. Clip the curves and press the seams open. Turn the velour pants right side out, so that the white pants are tucked inside as a lining. Baste together the waist edges of the white and velour pants, close to the edges.

Figure V

5. Turn the bodice assembly wrong side out and pin it to the pants assembly, placing right sides together and aligning the lower edge of the bodice with the waist edge of the pants. The center back opening of the bodice should fall at the center of the pant waist edge on either the front or the back (it doesn't matter which, because they're both the same — the center is what's important). Stitch the seam all the way around the waist edge, clip the curves, and then press the seam allowances toward the pants.

6. Dress Queenie in her suit, and tie the ribbons together at the back neck opening. Cut two 18-inch lengths of ribbon. Wrap one ribbon around the top of each skate boot and tie it in a bow at the front.

Making the Skirt

1. Each Skirt piece is a complete circle with a hole in the middle. Cut straight across each Skirt piece from the outer edge to the inner edge, as shown in **Figure U**.

2. Place two of the Skirt pieces right sides together, aligning the cut lines that you made in step 1. Stitch the two pieces together in a straight seam, ½ inch from one side of the cut line, as shown in **Figure V**. Press the seam open.

3. Open out the two Skirt pieces that are stitched together, and place the assembly right side up on a flat surface. Place the third Skirt piece right side down on top, aligning the short straight edge formed by the cut line with one end of the double assembly, and stitch the seam as you did in step 2 (**Figure W**). Press the seam open.

4. Fold the skirt assembly in half, placing right sides together, and stitch the two remaining free ends together as you did the seams in steps 2 and 3. Press the seam open. You should now have a very large circular skirt with a large hole for the waist in the middle.

5. Press a narrow hem to the wrong side of the skirt around the entire outer edge. Stitch the hem by machine.

6. Use the Skirt Binding Strip to encase the waist edge of the skirt, following the same procedures as you did to bind the neck edge of the bodice. The only difference will be that there is no back opening, as there was on the bodice, so simply overlap the ends of the Skirt Binding Strip, and finish the end that will show by turning it under.

7. Slip the finished skirt up over Queenie's legs; it should fit around her waist so that it doesn't fall down. If it is too large, take a small tuck at the center back. You can tack the skirt to the suit or leave it unattached.

Making the Skates

1. Cut the wooden dowel rod into four 3-inch lengths. (Because the dowel is so small, you should be able to do this using a sharp pocket knife or utility knife.) These short lengths of dowel will serve as the skate axles.

2. Install a wheel over each end of one dowel axle, and glue the wheels in place. The ends of the axle should be flush with the outer sides of the wheels. Attach two wheels to each of the remaining axles in the same manner.

3. Glue or whipstitch two axle-and-wheel assemblies to the bottom of each of Queenie's skate boots, one near the front and one near the back.

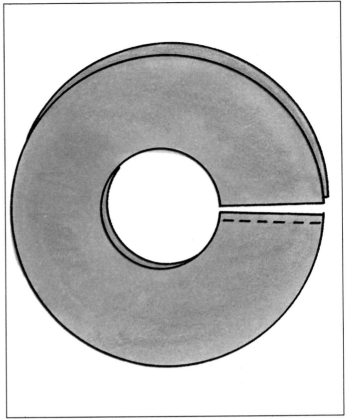

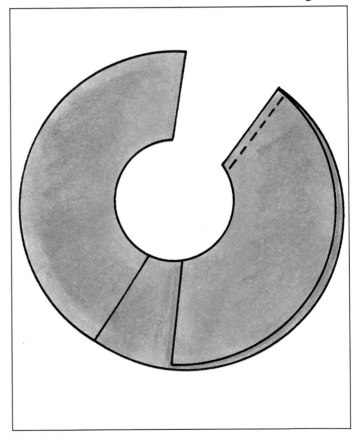

Piggy Bank

This unique Piggy Bank will be a prized addition to anyone's collection. It is easy to assemble, and can be stitched up in a short time. Overall dimensions are 5 x 8 inches.

Materials

One pair of pink regular-weave pantyhose
Scrap of black felt
1 yard of ⅜-inch-wide lavender satin ribbon
¾ yard of ⅜-inch-wide purple grosgrain ribbon
Three small silk flowers
3 yards of metallic elastic thread
Heavy-duty thread to match the hose; and a long sharp needle
½ bag of polyester fiberfill
White glue or hot-melt glue and a glue gun

Making the Body

1. Cut across the pantyhose at the top of the legs, as shown in **Figure A**. Remove the crotch.

2. Turn the panty wrong side out and stitch a seam across the lower open end.

3. Turn the panty right side out and lightly stuff it with a thin layer of fiberfill, so that you have a flat pad. Hold (or carefully pin) the top closed, and bring the ends of the pad together to form a hollow tube, as shown in **Figure B**. Pigs are supposed to be chubby, but this one needs to be trim enough to form an inside pocket for the coins. If more stuffing is needed, unroll the tube and add more fiberfill. When the pig is stuffed properly, whipstitch the upper edges of the panty together.

4. Re-form the hollow tube and whipstitch the ends together, leaving a 2-inch opening at the center for the coin slot, as shown in **Figure C**.

5. Run a line of basting stitches around one open end of the body tube. Pull the thread to gather the end and close it. Lock the stitch and cut the thread.

6. Repeat the procedures in step 5 to close the opposite end of the body tube.

7. To finish the coin opening, use metallic elastic thread and stitch around the opening, working buttonhole stitches. (See Tips & Techniques for buttonhole stitch illustration.)

Making the Head

Note: The head, nose, and feet each are made of a double layer of pantyhose so that they match the color of the body.

1. To make the head, cut two 6-inch-diameter circles from one leg of pantyhose. Wrap the circles around a 4-inch-diameter ball of fiberfill. Gather the raw edges of the hose and tie off the opening with thread. The tied-off portion of the hose will be positioned under the nose.

2. Use heavy-duty thread and a long sharp needle to sculpt the facial features. Follow the entry and exit points illustrated in **Figure D**.

   a. To create the eye indentations, enter at 1 and exit at 2. Reenter at 2 and exit at 3.

   b. Reenter at 3 and exit at 2. Pull the thread gently until eye indentations appear. Lock the stitch.

   c. To form the mouth, reenter at 2 and exit at 4.

Figure A

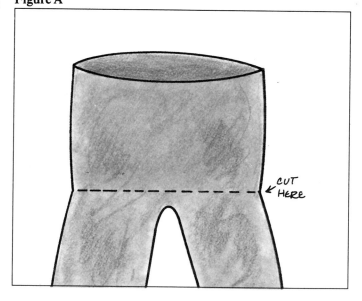

   d. Pull the thread across the surface, enter at 5, and exit at 2. Gently pull the thread until a top lip forms. Lock the stitch.

   e. Reenter at 2 and exit at 6. Pull the thread across the surface, enter at 7, and exit at 2. Gently pull the thread until a lower lip forms. Lock the stitch.

Figure B

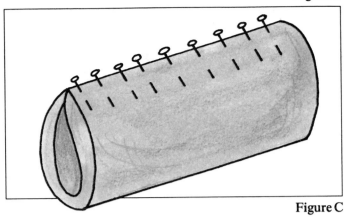

Figure C

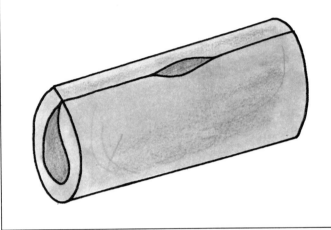

Figure D

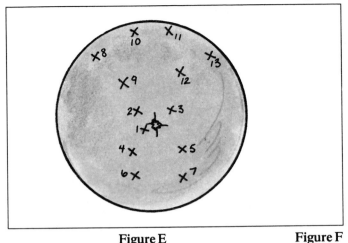

Figure E

Figure F

Figure G

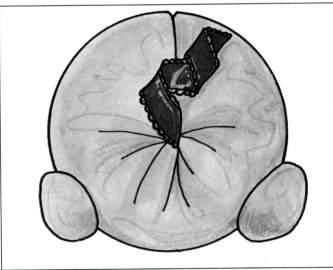

f. To form the ears, reenter at 2 and exit at 8.

g. Pull the thread across the surface, enter at 9, and exit at point 10.

h. Pull the thread across the surface, enter at 9, and exit at 2. Gently pull the thread until an ear forms, and then lock the stitch.

i. Repeat steps f through h at points 11, 12, and 13 to form the other ear. Exit at 2. Lock the stitch and cut the thread.

3. To form the nose, cut two 2-inch-diameter circles of pantyhose and wrap them around a small amount of fiberfill. Gather the raw edges, and tie them off, using thread. Follow the entry and exit points illustrated in **Figure E** to sculpt the nostrils.

a. Enter at 1 on the back and exit at 2.

b. Reenter at 2 and exit at 3.

c. Reenter at 3 and exit at 1. Gently pull the thread to form nostrils. Lock the stitch, but do not cut the thread.

4. Position the nose on the face so the top of the nose is at the eye line. Whipstitch the nose in place.

5. A full-size pattern for the Eyelash is provided in **Figure F.** Cut two Eyelashes from black felt and then glue one over each eye line.

6. Make four feet following the same instructions as you did in step 3 to make the nose. Whipstitch the feet to the body, positioning them so the pig will stand on his little feet and not on his little tummy.

Finishing

1. To make a tail, cut a 2-inch length of satin ribbon and glue one end to the gathered section at the rear of the pig. Curl the ribbon twice and glue the free end to the pig's back, as shown in **Figure G.**

2. Wrap the remaining satin ribbon, the grosgrain ribbon, and the metallic elastic thread, one at a time, around the neck and tie each one in a bow. Glue the flowers to the ribbon.

Gwendolyn Goosestop

Meet Gwendolyn, a whimsical stuffed goose who will stand guard to keep a door from slamming shut when your arms are fully loaded with cartons of eggs or glassware. She can be weighed down with rock salt, a brick, or other heavy material. Her plump body is approximately 12 inches long and 7 inches tall, and her neck and head are about 9 inches long, depending on how liberal you are with the stuffing.

Materials

One leg from a pair of nurse's white pantyhose
12-inch square of calico fabric for the bonnet
Three 12-inch squares of gold or orange felt
10-inch square of white eyelet fabric or plain white cotton fabric for the apron
3 x 26-inch rectangle of white cotton fabric for the apron tie
4-foot length of 1¼-inch-wide gathered white eyelet trim
18-inch length of 1-inch-wide grosgrain ribbon in a color to coordinate with the calico for the bonnet
Two black ½-inch-diameter shank-type buttons for the eyes
½ bag of polyester fiberfill

2-pound bag of rock salt, or a brick
11-inch length of ¾-inch-diameter wooden dowel rod
Heavy-duty white thread; a long sharp needle; and regular sewing thread to match the fabrics

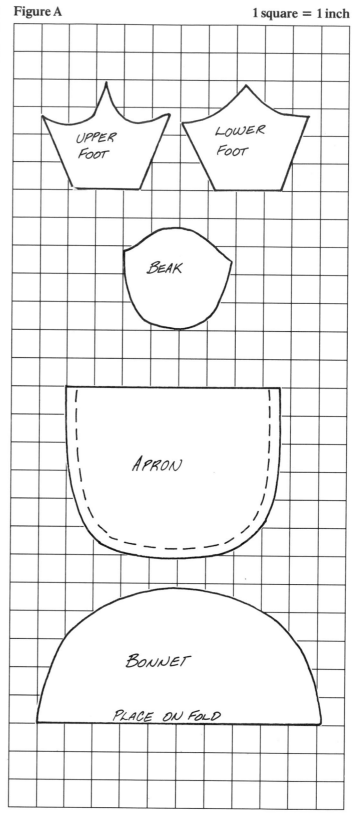

Figure A   1 square = 1 inch

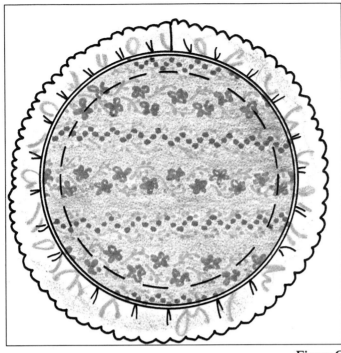

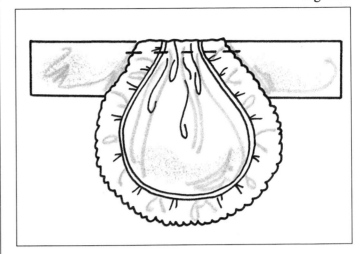

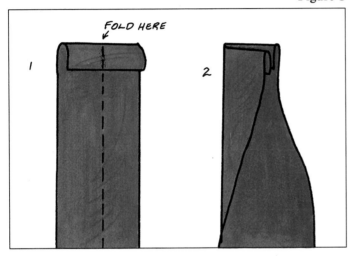

Figure C

2. Cut a 31-inch length of gathered eyelet trim. Pin the trim to the right side of the Bonnet piece, all the way around the outer edge, so that the eyelet extends out beyond the edge of the Bonnet piece. Overlap the ends of the trim and stitch the eyelet to the Bonnet piece.

3. Run a line of basting stitches around the Bonnet piece, 1 inch inside the eyelet-trimmed outer edge, as shown in **Figure B**. Do not cut the tails of thread. Place a fist-size ball of fiberfill in the center of the Bonnet piece, on the wrong side of the fabric, and pull the basting threads to gather the bonnet around the fiberfill until a 2½-inch-diameter opening remains. Tie off the gathering threads.

4. To create the bonnet ties, cut the grosgrain ribbon into two equal lengths. Finish one end of each ribbon tie by cutting a notch in it or by cutting it at an angle. Fold a narrow hem at the opposite end of one ribbon tie, and then fold the end in half lengthwise, as shown in **Figure C**. Whipstitch the folded end to the wrong side of the bonnet, just inside the gathers. Fold the unfinished end of the second ribbon tie in the same manner, and whipstitch it to the bonnet opposite the first one. This completes the bonnet.

5. To finish the lower edge of the Apron piece, press and stitch a narrow hem to the wrong side of the fabric all the way along the long curved edge. Do not hem the straight upper edge. Stitch the remaining length of gathered eyelet trim to the right side of the hemmed lower edge, as you did for the bonnet, so that the scalloped edge of the eyelet trim extends out beyond the edge of the Apron piece.

6. Baste close to the straight upper edge of the Apron piece and gather the fullness to a 5-inch length. Adjust the gathers evenly and baste over them to hold them in place.

7. The 3 x 26-inch piece of white cotton fabric will serve as the Apron Tie; place it right side up on a flat surface. Place the Apron piece right side down on top, aligning the gathered edge of the apron at the center of the long upper edge of the Tie. Stitch the seam, as shown in **Figure D**, turn the Tie piece upward along the stitching line, and press the seam allowances toward the Tie.

8. Fold the Tie in half lengthwise, placing right sides together. Stitch the seam across one end, then turn the corner and

Cutting the Pieces

Scale drawings for the Beak, Upper Foot, Lower Foot, Bonnet, and Apron are provided in **Figure A**. Enlarge the drawings to make full-size patterns, and cut the pieces listed below from the specified fabrics.

Gold Felt: Beak – cut two
              Lower Foot – cut two
              Upper Foot – cut two
White Eyelet Fabric: Apron – cut one
Calico: Bonnet – cut one

Making the Bonnet and Apron

1. Press a narrow hem to the wrong side of the calico Bonnet piece all the way around the outer edge, and stitch.

Figure E

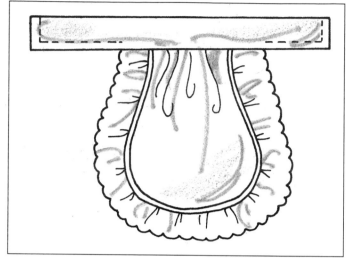

Figure G

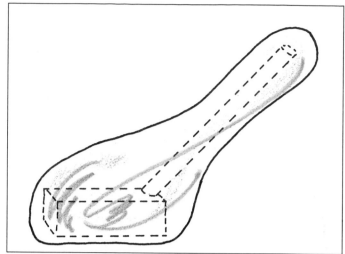

Figure F

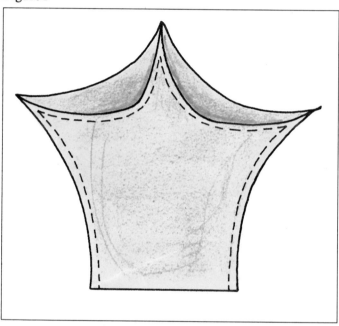

stitch along the aligned long raw edges, stopping when you get to the side edge of the apron, as shown in **Figure E**. Stitch the seam at the opposite end in the same manner, as shown.

9. Clip the corners and turn the tie right side out so that it encases the gathered edge of the apron. Press the seam allowance to the wrong side of the fabric along the unsewn center portion of the tie, which now should run along the wrong side of the apron. Whipstitch the pressed edge of the tie to the wrong side of the apron.

Making the Feet and Beak

1. Place the two Beak pieces together and stitch the seam along the long curved edge only, leaving the remaining edges open. This will be an outside seam, so trim the seam allowances close to the stitching line and do not turn the beak inside out. Stuff the beak with fiberfill. This completes the beak.

2. Place one Upper Foot piece and one Lower Foot piece together, matching the straight side edges and the short straight back edges. The scalloped (webbed) front edges of the two pieces will not match; allow the Lower Foot piece to extend beyond the Upper Foot piece along this edge. Stitch the two pieces together along both side edges and the scalloped front edge, following the outline of the Upper Foot piece, as shown in **Figure F**. Leave the short straight back edge open. Like the beak, these are outside seams, so do not turn the foot inside out. Stuff the foot lightly with fiberfill.

3. Repeat the procedures described in step 2 to create a second foot for Gwendolyn, using the remaining Upper and Lower Foot pieces.

Making the Body

1. Cut one leg from the white pantyhose at the panty line. Stuff the toe portion with fiberfill to form Gwen's head.

2. Wrap and glue fiberfill around the length of dowel rod and insert it into the pantyhose leg, all the way up into the stuffed head portion. Stuff additional fiberfill into the hose around the dowel rod to form the long neck, keeping the fiberfill as smooth as possible. The neck and head portion should be about 10 inches long. When you have finished stuffing the neck, continue to stuff the hose, using more fiberfill to create a plumper chest and shoulder area of the body.

3. Wrap and glue fiberfill around the unopened bag of rock salt or around the brick, and carefully insert it into the pantyhose leg. The dowel rod should rest against the top of the weight, as shown in **Figure G**. Stuff fiberfill around all sides of the bag or brick, so that the weight does not touch the pantyhose anywhere. Continue to stuff the hose and manipulate it to form the body, as shown.

4. Pull the open edge of the pantyhose leg to the underside of the body, gather it together, and whipstitch it closed.

Final Assembly

1. Cut a rectangular piece of gold felt to fit the bottom of Gwendolyn's body, and temporarily place the goose body on top of the felt rectangle. Place the two feet at one side of

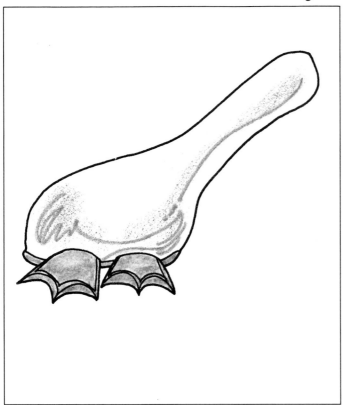

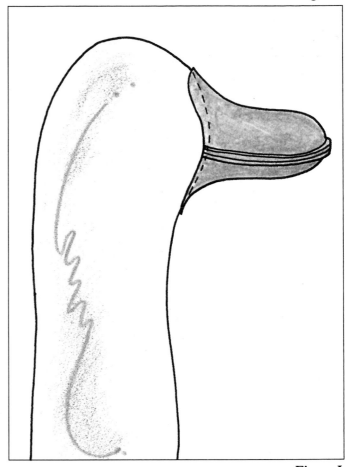

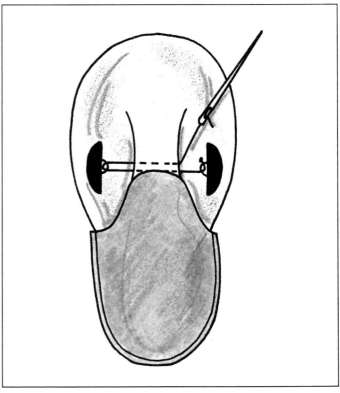

the body (not at the front), so that the webbed front of each foot extends outward from the body (**Figure H**). The open back edge of each foot should be inserted about ½ inch between the body and the felt bottom piece. Mark the placement of the feet on the felt bottom piece, remove the goose body, and glue or whipstitch the back of each foot to the felt piece. Reposition and glue the felt piece to the bottom of Gwen's body.

2. Place the beak against the front of the head, as shown in **Figure I**, and glue or whipstitch it in place.

3. Use a long sharp needle and heavy-duty white thread to sculpt the eye indentations on Gwen's face. Pinch up a vertical ridge in the center of the face, just above the beak. Stitch back and forth under the ridge one time, entering and exiting where you want the the eye indentations to appear. Now stitch underneath the ridge a second time, passing the needle through the shank of an eye button on each side, as shown in **Figure J**. Exit at the entry point on one side, pull the thread to indent the eyes, lock the stitch, and cut the thread.

4. Use the tip of the needle to lift fiberfill in the cheek areas, making them more rounded.

5. Put Gwen's bonnet on her head, bring the ribbon ties to the underside of her neck, and tie them in a bow behind her beak. Place the apron against the front of her chest, bring the apron ties around the base of her neck, and tie them in a large bow on top.

6. It may seem strange that Gwen's feet extend from the side of her body, but she will look just right if you arrange her correctly. Place her on the floor beside an open door, so that her feet are on the side facing away from the door. Turn her neck and head so they face in the same direction as her feet.

Christmas Wreath

This unique wreath is decorated with five holiday creations: Santa, a reindeer, a snowman, a mouse-in-a-stocking, and a candy cane that looks good enough to eat. The ornaments also can be used as tree decorations. Although this wreath is surprisingly easy and inexpensive to make, the abundance of lace, ribbon, and crisp green fabric makes it look quite luxurious. Overall size is 21 inches in diameter.

Materials

For the wreath:
14-inch-diameter polystyrene foam wreath form
2 yards of 36-inch-wide green cotton fabric
4 yards of 1½-inch-wide white lace trim
4 yards of 1½-inch-wide red grosgrain ribbon

For Santa:
6-inch-diameter circle of flesh-tone pantyhose
8-inch square of red felt
Scraps of green and white felt
One small red pompom
Black fine-point felt-tip marker
Two black-headed straight pins
One red-headed straight pin

For the reindeer:
5-inch square of shirt cardboard
Seat portion cut from a pair of brown pantyhose
Scrap of red felt
Scrap of red pantyhose for the nose
Two shiny silver shank-type buttons, ⅜ inch in diameter, for the eyes
Scrap of green felt
Three red-headed straight pins
One red chenille stem, 12 inches long

For the candy cane:
3½ x 9-inch rectangle of white pantyhose
One red chenille stem, 12 inches long
10-inch length of ⅜-inch-wide green grosgrain ribbon with white pin dots

For the mouse:
10-inch square of red pantyhose
9-inch square of white pantyhose
Small pink pompom
12-inch length of ⅜-inch-wide green grosgrain ribbon with white pin dots
Two black-headed straight pins

For the snowman:
5-inch square of white pantyhose
Five black-headed straight pins
Scraps of black, orange, and yellow felt
5-inch length of ¼-inch-wide red ribbon

Miscellaneous:
Heavy-duty brown thread; a long sharp needle; thread to match the fabrics; cosmetic cheek blusher; and about ¼ bag of polyester fiberfill

Covering the Wreath Base

1. Cut two strips from the green cotton, each 16 inches wide and 2 yards long. Place the strips right sides together, stitch across one short end, and press the seam open. You should now have a very long strip 16 inches wide.

2. Pin the length of lace trim to the right side of the green strip, along one long edge. The bound edge of the lace should be even with the fabric edge, and the scalloped edge of the lace should extend toward the center of the strip, as shown in **Figure A**. Baste the lace in place close to the bound edge.

3. Fold the strip in half lengthwise, right sides together. (The lace will be sandwiched between the two fabric layers.) Stitch a ¼-inch seam along the aligned long raw edges. Turn the resulting tube right side out and press.

4. Pin together the two fabric layers along the entire length of the tube, 5½ inches from the long folded edge. Cut across the foam wreath base, removing a small slice, as shown in **Figure B**, and check to make sure that the 5½-inch-wide casing will fit around the circumference of the wreath base. Adjust the width of the casing, if necessary, by moving the pins. Topstitch

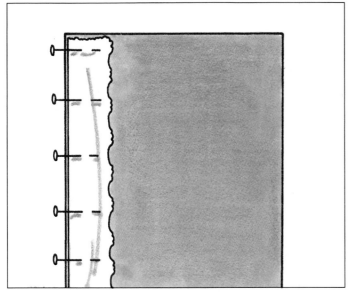

Figure C

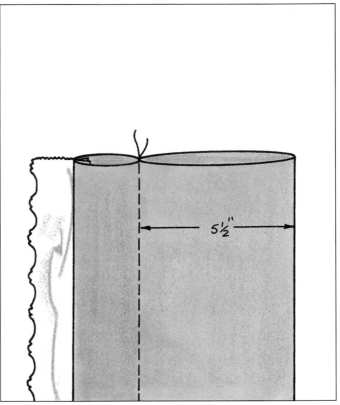

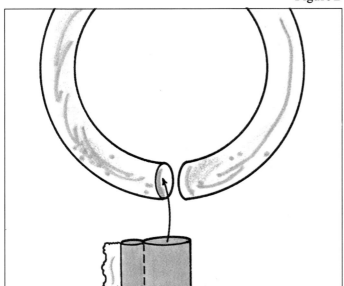

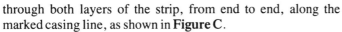

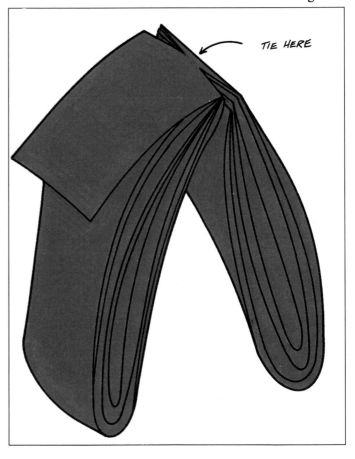

TIE HERE

through both layers of the strip, from end to end, along the marked casing line, as shown in **Figure C**.

5. Slide the casing around the wreath, so that the lace edge faces outward. Work the casing all the way around the wreath, adjusting the fullness evenly.

6. Hem the two raw ends of the casing and then whipstitch or blind stitch them together.

Adding the Bow

1. Cut an 18-inch length of red grosgrain ribbon and set it aside. Wrap the remaining length of ribbon into a continuous loop, approximately 8 inches in diameter.

2. Fold the wrapped loop of ribbon in half and clip at the fold on each side, as shown in **Figure D**. Be careful not to cut the ribbon in half. Tie the ribbon securely at the cut marks, using a piece of string.

Figure E

Figure F

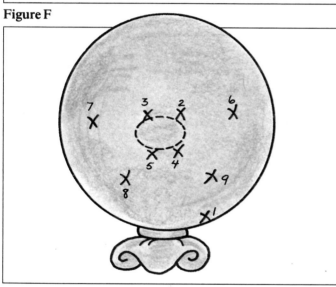

3. Twist, pull, and turn out each loop of ribbon, one at a time, until a full bow is formed.

4. Fold the 18-inch length of ribbon into a triangle at the center, as shown in **Figure E**. Glue or whipstitch the folded ribbon to the wreath. Place the bow on top of the triangle, and glue or whipstitch it to the wreath.

Assembling Santa

1. Wrap the 6-inch-diameter circle of pantyhose around a 4-inch-diameter ball of fiberfill. Gather the raw edge of the hose and tie it off, using thread.

2. Use a long sharp needle and heavy-duty brown thread to soft-sculpt the nose, following the entry and exit points illustrated in **Figure F**.

a. Enter at 1 and exit at 2. Sew a circle of basting stitches approximately ½ inch in diameter, exiting at 3.
b. Use the tip of the needle to carefully lift the fiberfill within the circle just enough to make a small bulge. Gently pull the thread until a nice round nose appears.
c. Lock the stitch under the bridge of the nose, exiting at point 2.
d. To form the nostrils, reenter at 2 and exit at 5.
e. Reenter ¼ inch above 5 and exit at 2.
f. Reenter at 2 and exit at 4.
g. Reenter ¼ inch above 4 and exit at 2. Lock the stitch under the bridge of the nose, exiting at 2.

3. To form the eyes and mouth, continue to follow the entry and exit points illustrated in **Figure F**.

a. To form the eyes, reenter at 2 and exit at 6.
b. Pull the thread across the surface, enter at 2, and exit at point 3.
c. Reenter at 3 and exit at 7.
d. Pull the thread across the surface, enter at 3, and exit at 2. Gently pull the thread until the closed eyes appear. Lock the stitch, exiting at 2.
e. To form the mouth, reenter at 2 and exit at 8.
f. Pull the thread across the surface, enter at 9, and exit at 3. Pull the thread until a smile appears, lock the stitch, and cut the thread.

4. Use the felt-tip marker to draw a tiny solid circle in the center of the mouth, and in the center of each eye line.

5. A full-size pattern for Santa's Hat is provided in **Figure G**. Cut the Hat piece from red felt.

6. Fold the Hat piece right sides together and stitch a ¼-inch-wide seam along the long straight edge.

7. Turn the hat right side out and glue it to the top of the head, placing the seam at the back.

8. Glue the red pompom to the tip of the hat.

9. Cut a ½ x 7-inch piece of white felt. Glue the felt strip around the lower edge of the hat, overlapping the ends at the back. Fold the tip of the hat to the side and glue it in place.

10. To form Santa's beard, glue a 3-inch-wide strip of fiberfill across the lower portion of the face. Separate the fiberfill to uncover the mouth. Shape the beard by fluffing the fiberfill.

11. Glue a small amount of fiberfill to the face above each eye to form the eyebrows.

12. A full-size pattern for the Holly Leaf is provided in **Figure H**. Cut two Leaves from green felt and glue them to the white felt strip on the hat. Insert two red-headed straight pins into the holly leaves, and glue them in place.

13. The completed Santa is shown in **Figure I**. Insert two black-headed straight pins into the dots on the eye lines to form Santa's eyes, and glue them in place. Glue one red-headed pin into the center of the mouth. Add a little color to Santa's cheeks and nose using cosmetic blusher.

Assembling the Reindeer

1. A full-size pattern for the Reindeer Head is provided in **Figure G**.

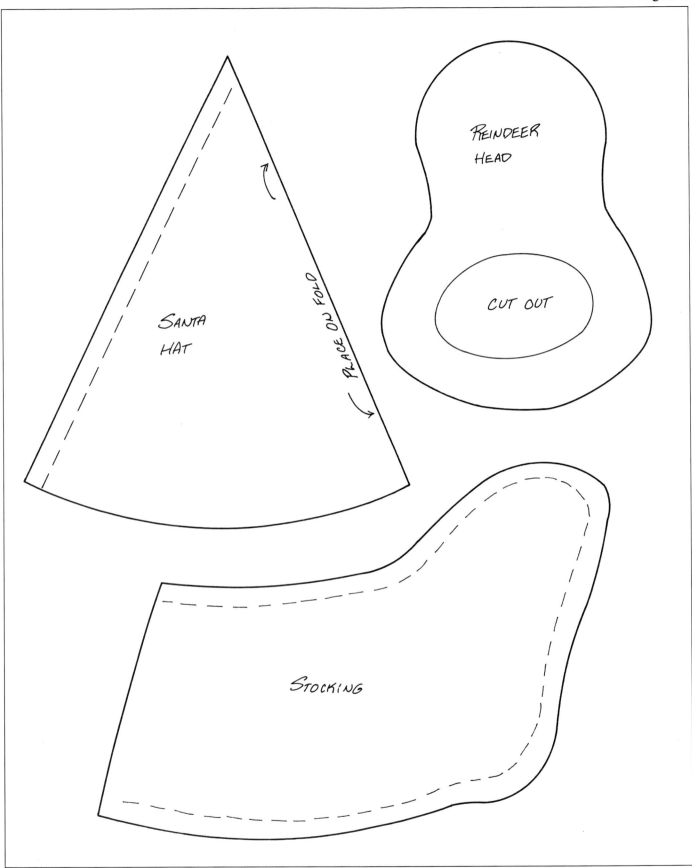

Santa Hat

Reindeer Head

CUT OUT

PLACE ON FOLD

Stocking

Figure H

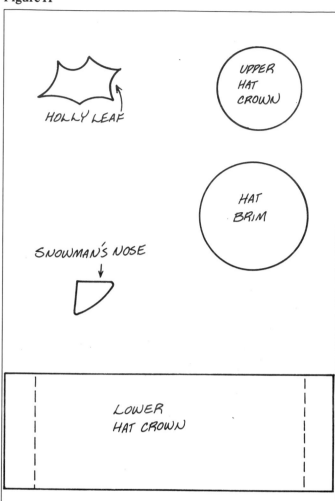

HOLLY LEAF

UPPER HAT CROWN

HAT BRIM

SNOWMAN'S NOSE

LOWER HAT CROWN

Figure I

Figure J

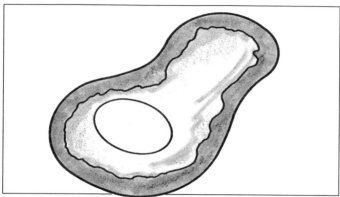

Figure K

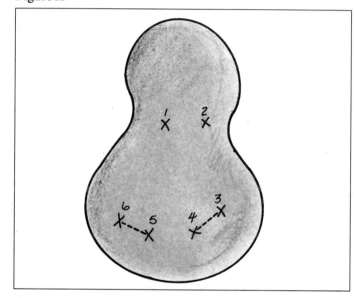

2. Cut one Reindeer Head from cardboard and cut a hole in the center, as indicated on the pattern.

3. Cut a 4 x 5-inch rectangle of brown pantyhose. Place the rectangle on a flat surface, and place the cardboard Reindeer Head piece on top. Fold the edges of the pantyhose rectangle around the edge of the cardboard and glue them in place (**Figure J**). Trim off the excess pantyhose.

4. Stuff the head with fiberfill, working through the center hole in the cardboard, until the hose is plumped out from the cardboard approximately 1½ inches.

5. Follow the entry and exit points illustrated in **Figure K** to sculpt the eyes and mouth, using a long sharp needle and heavy-duty thread.

    a. To form the eyes, enter at 1 and exit at 2.

    b. Reenter at 2 and exit at 1. Pull the thread gently to form a plump ridge in the center of the face. Lock the stitch.

    c. To form the mouth, reenter at 1 and exit at 3.

    d. Pull the thread across the surface, enter at 4, and exit at point 5.

    e. Pull the thread across the surface, enter at 6, and exit at point 2.

    f. Pull the thread until small mouth indentations appear. Lock the stitch and cut the thread.

Figure L

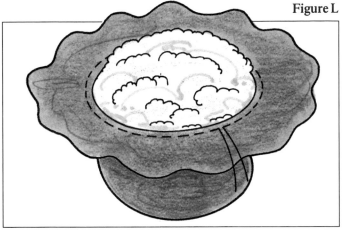

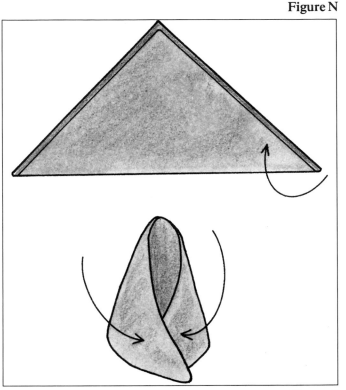

6. To make the nose, cut a 1½-inch-diameter circle of red pantyhose. Sew a 1-inch-diameter circle of basting stitches in the center of the hose. Place a small amount of fiberfill in the center of the basted circle, and pull the thread to encase the fiberfill (**Figure L**). Cut off the excess hose, and whipstitch the nose to the face, centered just above the two mouth lines.

7. Sew a shiny silver button over each eye line depression.

8. Twist the red chenille stem, as shown in **Figure M**, to form the reindeer's antlers, and glue them to the back of the head.

9. To form the ears, cut two 3-inch squares of brown pantyhose. Fold one square in half diagonally, and then fold the resulting triangle in half again to form an ear (**Figure N**). Tie off the bottom.

10. Repeat the procedures described in step 9, using the remaining square of pantyhose, to form a second ear.

11. Glue one ear to each side of the reindeer's head, below the antlers.

12. Cut green felt holly leaves as you did for Santa, and glue them to the top of the head. Glue red-headed straight pins into the leaves to serve as holly berries.

13. To make the bow tie, cut two rectangles from red felt: one 1¼ x 2¼ inches, and one ⅜ by 1¼ inches. Wrap the smaller rectangle around the center of the larger one, as shown in **Figure O**, and glue the ends together at the back. Glue the bow tie to the bottom center of the reindeer head.

Assembling the Candy Cane

1. Cut a 3 x 8-inch rectangle from white pantyhose. Fold the rectangle in half lengthwise, and stitch a ¼-inch-wide seam along the long edges and across one short end. Leave the opposite short end open. Turn the tube right side out.

2. Stuff the tube lightly with fiberfill. Fold the raw edges to the inside at the open end and whipstitch them together.

3. Twist the red chenille stem around the tube to create a spiral candy cane stripe, and secure each end using a spot of glue. Bend one end of the tube into a cane shape. Wrap the green ribbon around the middle of the cane and tie a bow at the front.

Figure P

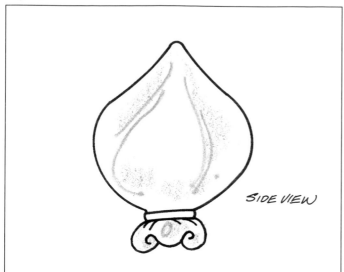

SIDE VIEW

Figure Q

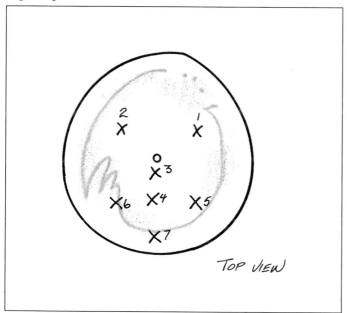

TOP VIEW

Figure R

Figure S

Making the Mouse

1. A full-size pattern for the Stocking is provided in **Figure G**. Cut two Stocking pieces from red pantyhose.

2. Sew the two Stocking pieces right sides together, leaving the top open and unstitched. Turn the stocking right side out.

3. Stuff the stocking lightly with fiberfill to within ½ inch of the top. Turn the raw edges to the inside around the top.

4. Cut a 5-inch-diameter circle of white pantyhose and wrap it around a 3-inch-diameter ball of fiberfill. Gather the raw edge of the hose and tie it off, using thread. This is the mouse's head.

5. Shape the pantyhose ball into a point at the top center, as shown in **Figure P**.

6. Follow the entry and exit points illustrated in **Figure Q** to sculpt the mouse's facial features, using a long sharp needle and heavy-duty thread.

a. To form the eye indentations, enter at the tied area on the bottom, and exit at 1. Reenter at 1 and exit at 2.

b. Reenter at 2 and exit at 1. Pull the thread until a ridge forms between the two points. Lock the stitch, exiting at point 1.

c. Reenter at 1 and exit at 3. Pull the thread across the surface, enter at 4, and exit at 2.

d. To form the mouth, reenter at 2, and exit at 5. Pull the thread across the surface, enter at 6, and exit at 1. Gently pull the thread until a mouth line appears. Lock the stitch, exiting at 1.

e. To form the lower lip, reenter at 1 and exit at 7. Reenter at 7 and exit at 1. Pull the thread until a lower lip appears. Lock the stitch and cut the thread.

7. Glue a pink pompom to the end of the nose.

8. To create an ear, cut a 2-inch-diameter circle of white pantyhose and wrap it around a ½-inch-diameter ball of fiberfill. Tie off the pantyhose edge and flatten the ball to form an ear, as shown in **Figure R**.

9. Repeat the procedures described in step 8 to make another ear. Brush cosmetic blusher in the center of each ear, and whipstitch them to the back of the head as shown in **Figure S**.

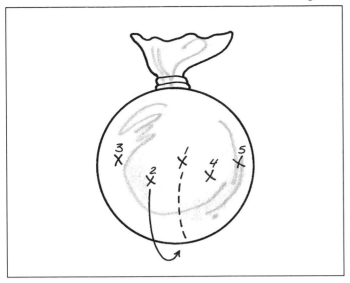

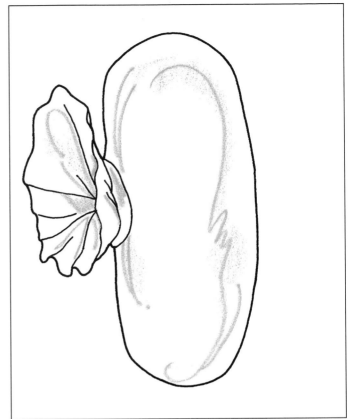

10. Use the black felt-tip marker to dot freckles on the lower portion of each cheek. Brush cosmetic blusher on the upper portion of each cheek and the lower lip. Glue or tack a few brown-thread "whiskers" to each cheek.

11. To create the paws, cut a 2-inch-diameter circle of white pantyhose and wrap it around a 1-inch-diameter ball of fiberfill. Tie off the pantyhose.

12. To sculpt the paws, follow the entry and exit points illustrated in **Figure T**.

    a. To separate the ball into two paws, enter at 1 and push the needle straight through the ball, exiting opposite point 1. Wrap the thread around the outside of the ball, enter at 1, and exit opposite 1 again. Pull the thread to separate the halves, and lock the stitch.

    b. Reenter at 1 and exit at 2. Follow the same procedures to divide each paw into three separate toes, taking slightly shorter stitches at points 2, 3, 4, and 5.

    c. Reenter at 5 and exit at the knot. Cut the thread.

13. Glue the paws underneath the front of the head, and glue the assembled head-and-paws into the open top of the stocking. Wrap the green grosgrain ribbon around the top of the stocking and tie a bow at the front.

Assembling the Snowman

1. Cut a 6-inch-diameter circle of white pantyhose. Wrap it around a 3-inch-diameter ball of fiberfill and tie off the hose.

2. Flatten and manipulate the ball to form a fat cigar-shaped roll, about 3½ inches long. The tied portion should be centered on the roll, as shown in **Figure U**.

3. To divide the snowman into three sections (head, upper body, and lower body), wrap heavy-duty thread around the body in two places and pull tightly, as shown in **Figure V**. The lower body should be slightly larger than the upper body, and the head should be only half the size of the upper body. Tie off the thread at the back, where the hose is tied. Slightly flatten the snowman.

4. To sculpt the snowman's eyes and mouth, follow the entry and exit points illustrated in **Figure W**.

Figure V

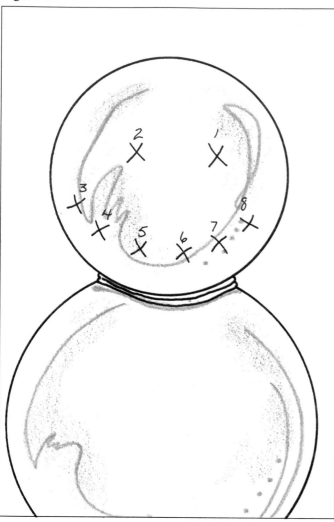

Figure X

a. Enter on the back of the head and exit at 1. Reenter at 1 and exit at 2. Reenter at 2 and exit at 1. Pull the thread gently to form indentations for the eyes. Lock the stitch at point 1.

b. To form the mouth, reenter at 1 and exit at 3. Reenter at 3 and exit at 8. This forms the outside edges of the mouth. Work from the outside in, alternating sides, as you follow the instructions in step c.

c. Reenter at 8 and exit at 4. Reenter at 4 and exit at 7. Reenter at 7 and exit at 5. Reenter at 5 and exit at 6. Reenter at 6 and exit at 2. Reenter at 2 and exit on the back of the head.

d. Pull the thread gently until the mouth points appear. Lock the stitch and cut the thread.

5. Use the black felt-tip marker to make a dot on each of the mouth points, and three dots down the center front of the upper body. Insert and glue black-headed straight pins into each eye depression, and into each dot along the center front of the upper body section.

6. To make the scarf, cut a 1 x 6-inch rectangle of yellow felt and wrap it around the snowman's neck, forming a half knot at the front.

7. A full-size pattern for the Snowman's Nose is provided in **Figure H**. Cut one Nose from orange felt and glue it to the snowman's face. The snowman is shown in **Figure X**.

8. Full-size patterns for the hat pieces are provided in **Figure H**. Cut one Lower Hat Crown, one Upper Hat Crown, and one Brim from black felt.

9. Wrap the Lower Hat Crown into a cylinder, overlapping and glueing together the two end seam allowances. Center and glue the Upper Hat Crown over one open end of the cylinder. Center and glue the Brim over the other open end.

10. Glue the length of red ribbon around the crown, just above the brim, overlapping the ends at the center back.

11. Glue the hat to the snowman's head (**Figure Y**).

Final Assembly

Arrange the reindeer, snowman, Santa, candy cane, and mouse around the wreath. When you find the arrangement that pleases you, tack or glue each item to the wreath. Attach a loop of ribbon or string to the top of the wreath, on the back, so that you can hang it.

Materials

One pair of adult-size white athletic tube socks

⅜ yard of 36-inch-wide cotton fabric for the beanbags (We used a burgundy-colored fabric with white pin dots.)

Two 5 x 10-inch rectangles of heavy-weight tight-weave fabric to hold the weights (Color doesn't matter, as this fabric will be inside the beanbags.)

2 yards of ⅜-inch-wide grosgrain ribbon (We used blue ribbon with white pin dots.)

1¼ yards of ¾-inch-wide white lace trim

½ bag of polyester fiberfill

Heavy-duty white thread; thread to match the beanbag fabric; and a long sharp needle

One white chenille stem

Cosmetic cheek blusher

Black acrylic paint and a medium-tip artist's paint brush, or a permanent-ink black felt-tip marker

4 pounds of smooth clean stones, marbles, or something similar for the weights

Making the Piggy's Head

1. Stuff the toe section of one tube sock with fiberfill until it is about 4 inches in diameter. Tie off the neck, using heavy-duty thread, and cut off the excess sock fabric about 3 inches below the tied neck.

2. To sculpt the facial features, use heavy-duty white thread and a long sharp needle. Follow the entry and exit points illustrated in **Figure A**.

   a. Enter at 1 behind the knot, push the needle through the head, and exit at 2.

   b. To make the snout, sew a clockwise oval of basting stitches; the oval should be about 2 inches in diameter crosswise, and about 1 inch in diameter vertically. Exit at 3. Lift the fiberfill within the oval, using the tip of the needle, and then pull the thread gently until the snout appears. Lock the stitch, exiting at 2.

   c. To make the nostrils, reenter at 2 and exit at 4. Reenter at 4 and exit at 3.

   d. Reenter at 3 and exit at 5. Reenter at 5 and exit at 2. Pull the thread gently until two nostril indentations appear, and lock the stitch at 2.

   e. To create the mouth, reenter at 2 and exit at 6. Pull the thread across the surface, enter at 7, and then exit at 8.

   f. Pull the thread across the surface, enter at 9, and exit at 7. Pull the thread across the surface, enter at 9, and exit at 2. Gently pull the thread until the mouth appears and lock the stitch at 2.

   g. To form the eyes, reenter at 2 and exit at 10. Pull the thread across the surface, enter at 2, and exit at 11.

   h. Pull the thread across the surface, enter at 3, and exit at 2. Lock the stitch at 2.

   i. To form one ear, reenter at 2 and exit at 12. Pull the thread across the surface, enter at 13, and exit at 14.

   j. Pull the thread across the surface, enter at 13, and exit at 2. Pull the thread until the ear appears and lock the stitch at 2.

Piggy Bookends

Your little ones will enjoy keeping their books neat and tidy between these adorable bookends. One features a piggy head and front feet, and the other features the piggy's posterior and back legs. Weighted beanbags provide support. We stuffed and sculpted athletic tube socks to create the piggy parts, but you can make them from heavy-weight white or pink pantyhose if you prefer.

Figure A

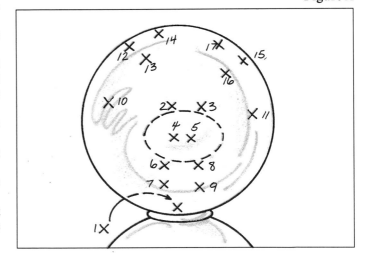

Figure B

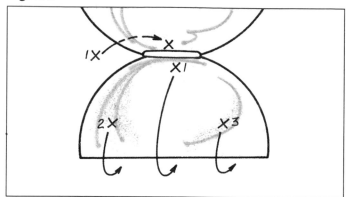

Figure C

Figure D

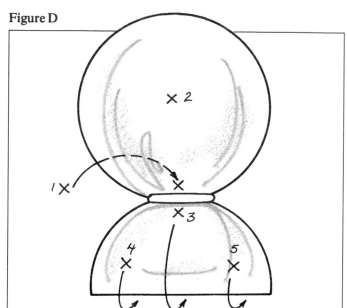

k. To sculpt the second ear, reenter at 2 and exit at 3. Reenter at 3 and exit at 15. Follow the same procedures as you did to form the first ear, using points 15, 16, and 17 shown in **Figure A**. Return the needle, underneath the surface, to point 3 and lock the stitch at 3.

l. Reenter at 3 and exit at 1. Do not cut the thread.

3. The feet are formed from the 3 inches of sock that you left under the neck knot. Stuff this portion of the sock with a small amount of fiberfill and flatten it slightly. Turn the open edge to the inside and whipstitch it closed. The foot portion should now look like the illustration in **Figure B**.

4. To sculpt the feet, follow the entry and exit points illustrated in **Figure B**, continuing with the same thread that you used to sculpt the facial features.

  a. Pull the thread around the outside of the foot portion, crossing the whipstitched edge of the sock, to the front. Enter at 1 (just below the knot) on the front, and exit at 1 on the back. Pull the thread to divide the stuffed portion of sock into two feet.

b. Reinforce the dividing line by repeating step a. Lock the stitch at 1 on the back.

c. To divide one foot into two toes, reenter at 1 on the back, push the needle under the surface, and then exit at 2 on the back.

d. Wrap the thread around the end of the foot, enter at 2 on the front, and exit at 2 on the back. Pull the thread to divide the two toes, and repeat the stitch to secure it. Lock the stitch at 2 on the back.

e. To divide the toes on the other foot, reenter at 2, push the needle under the surface, and exit at 3 on the back. Wrap the thread around the end of the foot, enter at 3 on the front and exit at 3 on the back. Pull the thread until the toes are divided, repeat the stitch, and then lock the stitch and cut the thread.

5. To finish the piggy's head and front feet, use black acrylic paint or a marker to color the toes, as shown in **Figure C**. Paint several straight lines under each sculpted eye line to create the eyelashes, and paint a small black dot in each sculpted nostril. When the paint has dried completely, brush cheek blusher lightly across the upper portion of the snout and across the front of each ear. Use the blusher more liberally to create two large cheek spots, and to create a small circle of color on the mouth.

Making the Piggy's Posterior

1. Stuff the toe portion of the remaining uncut tube sock until it is about 4 inches in diameter, and tie it off using heavy-duty thread. Cut off the unstuffed portion of the sock, leaving 3 inches below the knot for the back feet.

2. To sculpt the anatomical features and feet, follow the entry and exit points illustrated in **Figure D**, using heavy-duty white thread and a long sharp needle.

  a. Enter at 1, push the needle through the body, and exit at point 2.

  b. Pull the thread downward across the surface, enter at 1 on the front, and exit at 1 on the back. Pull the thread to divide the "cheeks." Lock the stitch at 1, but do not cut the thread.

3. Stuff the sock below the knot to create the back feet as you did for the front feet. Turn the open edge to the inside and whipstitch it closed.

4. To sculpt the feet, follow the entry and exit points illustrated in **Figure D**, continuing with the same thread that you used to divide the posterior. As you can see in **Figure D**, the procedures are the same as those used to sculpt the front feet.

5. To finish the posterior, paint the toes using black paint or a marker, as shown in **Figure E**. Apply blusher to each "cheek." To create the tail, wrap the chenille stem around a pencil as many times as it will go, and then remove the pencil. Glue and stitch one end of the tail to the piggy's posterior, at the top of the long vertical stitch, as shown in **Figure E**.

Making the Beanbags

1. Cut two 11 x 18-inch rectangles from the beanbag fabric.

2. Fold one of the rectangles in half widthwise, placing right sides together; you should now have a double-layered rectangle 9 x 11 inches. Stitch a ½-inch-wide seam along each 9-inch edge, and press both seam allowances in the same direction (not open) along each seam. Do not turn the assembly right side out.

3. For each of these seams, the end that is at the folded edge of the rectangle must be squared off, so the beanbag will fit squarely against the books. Grasp the fabric on each side of one seam, near the bottom corner, and separate the layers of fabric. Smooth the sewn corner flat against the bottom so the side seam is centered and the corner becomes a point, as shown in **Figure F**. Mark a 3-inch width horizontally across the fabric (there should be 1½ inches on each side of the center seam line), as shown in **Figure F**. Stitch a straight seam across the assembly, along the marked line. Trim the seam allowance to ¼ inch.

4. Square the opposite lower corner of the beanbag, following the instructions in step 3.

5. To finish the open upper edge of the sack, press a ¼-inch-wide hem to the wrong side of the fabric all the way around the upper edge. Turn the edge under again, so you have a doubled hem, and press.

6. Cut a 21-inch length of white lace trim and pin it to the wrong side of the beanbag around the pressed upper edge, so that the scalloped edge of the lace extends out beyond the edge of the beanbag. Overlap the ends, and stitch the lace in place.

7. Repeat steps 2 through 6 to make a second beanbag, using the remaining rectangle of fabric that you cut in step 1.

8. To make the smaller sacks that will contain the weights, use the 5 x 10-inch rectangles of heavy-weight fabric. Fold one of the rectangles in half widthwise; you should now have a double-layered 5 x 5-inch square.

9. Stitch a ¼-inch-wide seam along each side edge, leaving the remaining edge open. You may wish to double stitch these seams so they will not break under the weights.

10. Press the seam allowance to the wrong side of the fabric around the open end of the sack. Turn the sack right side out, and fill it with marbles or whatever you have chosen for weights. Whipstitch the opening edges together, going back and forth along the edge several times so the stitches will not break.

11. Repeat the procedures in steps 8 through 10 to make the second small sack.

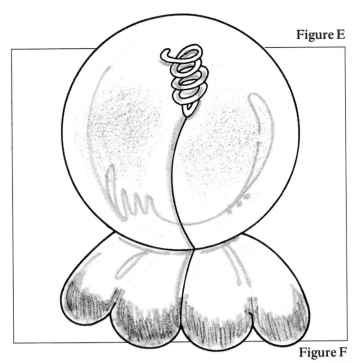

Figure E

Figure F

Final Assembly

1. Place one weighted sack inside one of the beanbags. Stuff fiberfill into the beanbag around and over the sack, leaving 1½ inches unstuffed at the top.

2. Use heavy-duty thread to run a line of basting stitches by hand all the way around the beanbag, about 1½ inches from the open upper edge; do not cut off the tails of thread. Place the head assembly on top of the beanbag and pull up the basting stitches to gather the sack snugly around it. Adjust the gathers evenly and tie off the threads. Glue and whipstitch the head assembly to the gathered portion of the beanbag.

3. Repeat the procedures described in steps 1 and 2 to assemble the piggy posterior, using the remaining sack and beanbag.

4. Cut a 2-foot length of ribbon and cut the ends at an angle. Wrap it around the gathered portion of the piggy head beanbag, hiding the stitches, and tie it in a bow at one side of the head. Cut another 2-foot length of ribbon, angle the ends, and wrap it around the gathered portion of the piggy posterior beanbag. Tie it in a bow at the top.

5. Cut a 1-foot length of ribbon, angle the ends, and wrap it around the front feet at the point where they meet the head. Tie the ends in a bow under the chin. Use the remaining ribbon to form a small bow and glue or tack it just under the tail.

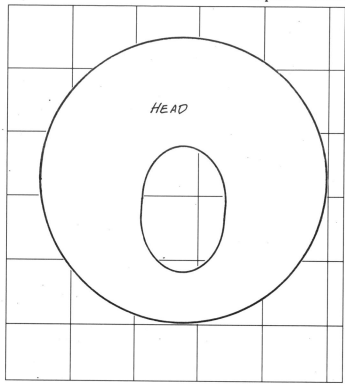

HEAD

Sock It Away

This unique little item will hold money, marbles, or whatever you want to sock away. It consists of a tube-sock body and a sculpted pantyhose face with an open mouth to accept your savings. You may be inspired to create an entire family of "Sock-Its" to help you save for those special purchases. Let your imagination run away with you and have fun while you're saving.

Making the Head

1. A scale drawing for the Head is provided in **Figure A**. Enlarge the drawing to make a full-size pattern.

2. Cut one Head piece from cardboard, and cut out the mouth area where indicated on the pattern.

3. Glue an even layer of fiberfill, about 1½ inches thick, to one side of the cardboard Head piece. Do not cover the mouth area with fiberfill.

4. Cut a 10-inch length from the center of the pantyhose leg, and insert the fiberfill-covered Head piece inside the pantyhose tube, as shown in **Figure B**.

5. To secure the pantyhose to the back (uncovered side) of the cardboard, simply glue the back open end of the pantyhose tube to the cardboard, around the outer edge, as shown in **Figure C**. Do not cover the mouth hole.

6. To create the open mouth, and secure the open end of the hose that is at the front (fiberfill-covered side) of the cardboard, stuff the front end of the pantyhose tube through the mouth hole in the cardboard, from front to back, and pull the hose through the hole. Pull firmly, smoothing out the pantyhose "skin" on the front of the face. Trim most of the excess hose, and glue the edge of the hose to the back of the cardboard, around the edge of the mouth.

Sculpting the Face

1. Follow the entry and exit points illustrated in **Figure D** to form the eyes and mouth, using a long sharp needle and heavy-duty brown thread.

Materials

One leg of regular-weave flesh-tone pantyhose
One large tube sock
Two ½-inch-diameter shank-type buttons for the eyes
A small amount of polyester fiberfill
4½-inch-diameter embroidery hoop (We chose red to coordinate with our tube sock.)
3-foot length of yarn for the hair
4 x 6-inch rectangle of felt for the bow tie
Heavy-duty brown thread; a long sharp needle; and white glue or hot melt glue and a glue gun
5-inch square of stiff cardboard
12-inch length of ribbon or string for the hanger
Cosmetic cheek blusher

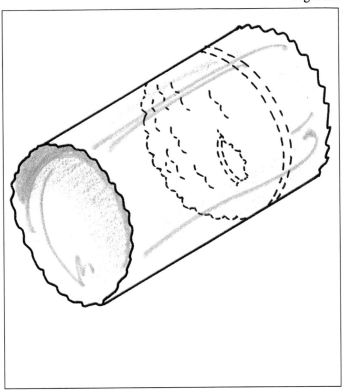

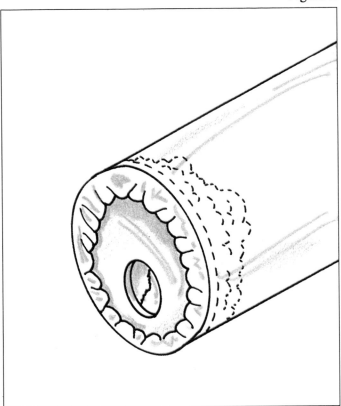

a. Each eye consists of narrow upper and lower curved ridges. A button will be sewn to the face between the ridges for each eye. To form the left eye, enter at 1 and exit at 2.

b. Pinch up a curved ridge between 2 and 3. Stitch back and forth underneath the ridge, exiting at 3. Pull the thread gently until the curved ridge appears, and lock the stitch at 3.

c. Enter at 3 and exit at 4.

d. Pinch up a curved ridge between points 4 and 5, and stitch back and forth under the ridge, exiting at 5. Pull the thread and lock the stitch at 5.

e. To create the right eye, repeat the same procedures to form a ridge between points 6 and 7, and between points 8 and 9. Lock the stitch and cut the thread.

f. To form the mouth, pinch up a wider curved ridge between points 11 and 12.

g. Enter at 10 and exit at 11. Stitch back and forth under the ridge, exiting at 12. Pull firmly, lock the stitch, and cut the thread.

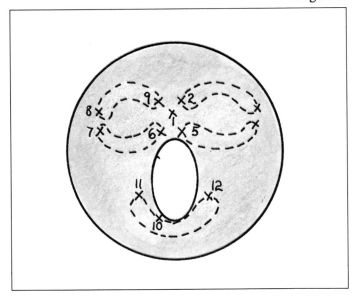

2. To create the nose, encase a 2-inch-diameter ball of fiberfill in a 4-inch-diameter circle of pantyhose. Gather the pantyhose edge around the fiberfill and tie it off, using heavy-duty thread. Trim off the excess hose below the knot. Manipulate the nose so that it is an oval shape, rather than round.

3. The finished face is shown in **Figure E**. Glue the nose to the face, placing the tied portion against the face. The upper end of the nose should lie between the eyes, and the lower end should cover the top of the mouth.

4. Stitch and glue the two blue buttons to the face, one between the ridges of each eye.

5. To create the hair, cut and glue short lengths of yarn to the top and sides of the face, as shown.

6. Brush cosmetic blusher over the cheeks and mouth to add a little color. The bow tie will be added later.

Final Assembly

1. Insert the top of the tube sock, and the center point of the 12-inch length of ribbon or string, between the sections of the embroidery hoop. Adjust the sock so that about 1 inch extends

above the hoop, and place the center of the ribbon or string so that it is opposite the hoop screw. Tighten the hoop screw, and fold the upper sock allowance to the inside.

2. Glue the finished head to the open side of the embroidery hoop and to the sock top allowance, as shown in **Figure F**. The head should be turned so that the top is aligned with the ribbon or string, and the chin is aligned with the hoop screw.

3. Tie the ends of the ribbon or string into a secure knot and bow, to create the hanger.

4. To make the bow tie, cut two rectangles of yellow felt: one 2½ x 4½ inches, and one 1 x 2 inches. Wrap the smaller rectangle around the center of the larger rectangle, overlapping the ends so that the larger rectangle is gathered at the center. Glue the ends of the smaller rectangle together. Glue the felt bow tie to the head and embroidery hoop so that it covers the hoop screw assembly.

Figure F

Materials

½ yard of lightweight stretch terry cloth

One leg of regular-weave flesh-tone pantyhose

½ bag of polyester fiberfill

Small section of wig (or substitute yarn) for the hair

Felt-tip markers in black and red

Cosmetic cheek blusher

Heavy-duty flesh-tone thread; a long sharp needle; and regular thread to match the terry cloth

20-inch length of yarn to match the terry cloth

Cutting the Pieces

1. Scale drawings for the Body, Back, and Hood are provided in **Figure A**. Enlarge the drawings to make full-size patterns.

2. Cut two Bodies, two Hoods, and one Back from the lightweight terry cloth.

Making the Body

1. Turn under and stitch a ¼-inch-wide hem along the straight lower edge of the Back, between the sleeves. Do not hem the lower edges of the sleeves.

2. The Back forms the opening into which you insert your hand to manipulate the puppet. Place one Body piece right side up on a flat surface. Place the Back right side down on top, aligning the sleeves and upper edges. Place the second Body piece right side down on top of the stack (**Figure B**).

3. Stitch the seams along the edges, leaving neck and sleeve openings, as shown in **Figure C**. (Remember to stretch the material gently as you sew, or use a stretch-stitch setting on your machine.) Clip the curves, and turn the body right side out.

4. Stuff the body with fiberfill from the feet up to the lower edge of the sleeve.

Baby-Doll Puppet

This cutie pie can wave bye-bye and move in an amazingly lifelike manner... with a little help from a friend. The back section is left unstuffed, so you can insert your hand into the puppet, and manipulate her little arms and head. She is approximately 15 inches long.

1 square = 1 inch   Figure A

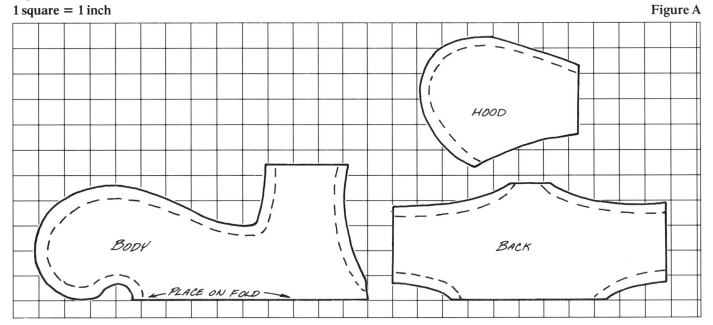

HOOD

BODY

← PLACE ON FOLD →

BACK

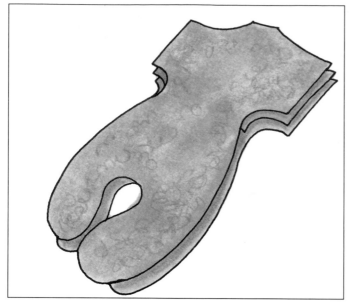

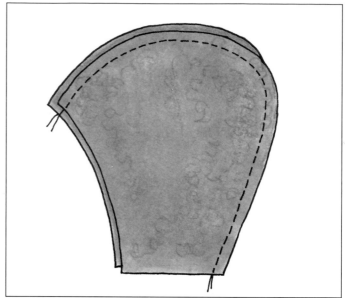

Figure C

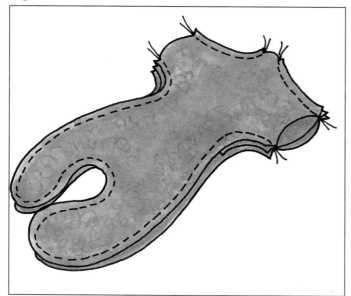

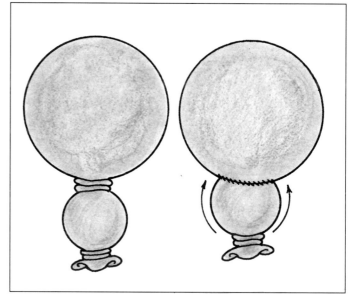

5. Place the Hood pieces right sides together and stitch the center back seam along the long curved edge (**Figure D**). Turn under a ¼-inch-wide hem around the face opening. The body and hood sections will be assembled later.

Making the Head

1. Tie a knot in one leg of pantyhose near the knee. Cut across the hose about 1 inch above the knot, and again about 10 inches below the knot. Turn the hose so that the knot is on the inside. Stuff with fiberfill until the head is approximately 3½ inches in diameter. Tie a knot at the neck, leaving the excess hose below the knot.

2. Add about 1½ inches of fiberfill under the knot for the neck stem. Tie the hose in a knot below the neck (**Figure E**). Cut off the excess hose below the lower knot.

3. Push the neck stem up to the base of the head. Secure the neck to the head with whipstitches all the way around.

4. To soft-sculpt the nose and eye features, follow the entry and exit points illustrated in **Figure F**.

   a. To form the nose, enter at 1, push the needle through the head, and exit at 2. Sew a clockwise circle of basting stitches, about 1 inch in diameter, and exit at 3.

   b. Gently pull the thread until a round nose appears. Use the tip of the needle to lift the fiberfill within the circle. Lock the stitch and exit at 2.

   c. To form the nostrils, reenter at 2 and exit at 4.

   d. Reenter ¼ inch above 4 and exit at 3.

   e. Reenter at 3 and exit at 5.

   f. Reenter about ¼ inch above 5 and exit at 2. Lock the stitch at 2.

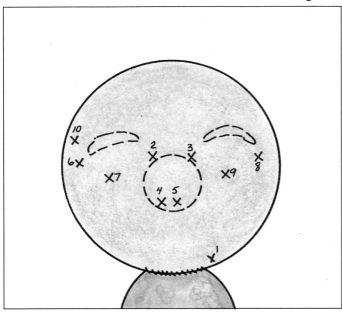

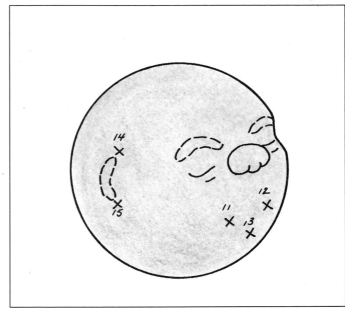

g. To sculpt one eye line, pull the thread across the surface, enter at 6, and exit at 7.

h. Reenter at 7 and exit at 2. Gently pull the thread until the eye line is formed. Lock the stitch.

i. Pinch up a narrow curved ridge over the left eye line. This will be the eyelid.

j. Reenter at 2, stitch back and forth under the eyelid ridge, and exit at 10.

k. Reenter at 10 and exit at 2. Pull the thread and lock the stitch at 2.

l. Repeat the procedures in steps g through k to soft-sculpt the opposite eye line and eyelid. Do not cut the thread.

5. To soft-sculpt the mouth and ears, continue with the same thread, following the entry and exit points that are illustrated in **Figure G**.

a. Reenter at 2 and exit at 11. Pull the thread across the surface, enter at 12, and exit at 13.

b. Reenter at 13 and exit at 2. Gently pull the thread until a mouth and lower lip appear. Lock the stitch.

c. To form one ear, reenter at 2 and exit at 14. Pinch up a small curved ridge on the side of the head.

d. Stitch back and forth underneath the ridge between points 14 and 15. Pull the thread until an ear appears.

e. Reenter at 15 and exit at 2. Lock the stitch.

f. Repeat steps c through e to form the opposite ear.

g. Reenter at 2, exit at 1, lock the stitch, and cut the thread.

6. Glue or whipstitch the section of wig (or yarn) to the top of the head, as shown in **Figure H**.

7. Use the black marker to draw the eyes; and the red marker to draw the lips.

Making the Hands

1. Cut a 2-inch circle of pantyhose, and wrap it around a 1-inch ball of fiberfill. Tie the hose together at the bottom using heavy-duty thread.

2. To soft-sculpt the fingers, follow the entry and exit points illustrated in **Figure I**.

a. Enter at 1 and exit at 2 (on what will be the back side of the hand).

b. Slightly flatten the hand at the top to form the finger portion of the fist. Wrap the thread around the end of the finger and insert the needle on the palm side of the fist directly opposite 2. Exit at 2 and pull the thread tightly to form the first finger.

c. Reenter at 2 and exit at 3 to begin the next finger.

d. Wrap the thread around the end of the finger and enter on the palm side directly opposite 3. Exit at 3 on the back. Pull the thread tightly to form the second finger.

Figure I

Figure J

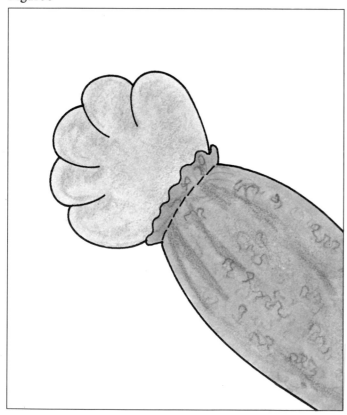

Figure K

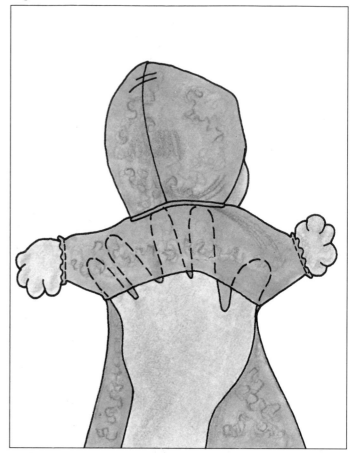

4. Insert the wrist end of one hand into one of the sleeve openings, positioned so the palm side of the hand faces forward. Turn the raw edges of the sleeve to the inside, and work a running stitch around the wrist, gathering the sleeve to fit, as shown in **Figure J**.

5. Repeat step 4 for the opposite hand.

Final Assembly

1. Insert the neck stem into the neck opening of the body. Turn under the raw edge around the neck opening and whipstitch it to the head, covering the line of stitches that secured the head to the neck stem.

2. Place the hood on the head and adjust it to your satisfaction. Turn under the raw lower edge of the hood and whipstitch it to the neck edge of the body and to the neck stem inside. Glue or whipstitch the hood around the face opening.

3. Wrap a 14-inch length of yarn around the neck and tie a bow at the front. Tie the remaining 6 inches of yarn in a small bow, and glue or whipstitch it to the top front of the hood.

4. Add a little color to Baby's cheeks, nose and eyelids using the cosmetic blusher.

5. To manipulate the puppet, place your hand underneath the back flap. Insert your thumb inside one arm and your little finger and ring finger into the other arm. Your index and middle fingers can manipulate the head. Find the hand position that is most comfortable for you (**Figure K**). Wrap the baby in a small blanket (to hide your hand). Cradle the puppet in your free arm.

e. Repeat these procedures at points 4 and 5 to form the last two fingers.

f. Reenter at 5 and exit at 1. Lock the stitch and then cut the thread.

3. Repeat steps 1 and 2 to form the other hand.

Materials

One lower leg of pink sandalfoot pantyhose
One leg of blue pantyhose
One small balloon
½ yard of white nylon net
One bunch of yellow silk buttercups
6-inch length of ⅛-inch-wide lavender satin ribbon
½ yard of ½-inch-wide lavender satin ribbon
A ¾-inch-diameter pale blue pompom
Two very tiny black beads
A small amount of polyester fiberfill
Heavy-duty light blue thread and a long sharp needle
Spray-on fabric starch
¾ yard of ¾-inch-wide white lace trim
One spray-can top

Making the Bunny

Each of the bunny's body parts (head, body, ears, feet, and haunches) are sculpted separately, then glued or sewn together to create the finished bunny. The head is sculpted first.

1. Cut a 5-inch-diameter circle from the leg of light blue hose, and wrap it around a 2-inch-diameter ball of fiberfill. Gather the edge of the hose and tie it off, using thread. Trim off the excess hose below the tied portion. Flatten the ball slightly, placing the knot at the back.

2. Follow the entry and exit points illustrated in **Figure A** to sculpt the facial features.
   - **a.** Enter through the knotted side, push the needle straight through the head, and exit at 1 on the front.
   - **b.** Reenter at 1 and exit at 2.
   - **c.** Reenter at 2 and exit at 3. Pull the thread until two small eye depressions appear. Lock the stitch at 3.
   - **d.** Sew a tiny circle of basting stitches, beginning and ending at 3. Use the tip of the needle to lift fiberfill within the circle, and pull the thread to form the nose. Lock the stitch at 3.

Easter Bunny Egg

You'll have to hunt high and low to find an Easter idea as clever and attractive as this. The egg is made of pantyhose shaped over a balloon form; it contains a tiny stuffed and sculpted bunny, a sprig of artificial flowers, and nylon net for a fluffy effect. Overall height is approximately 9 inches.

Figure A

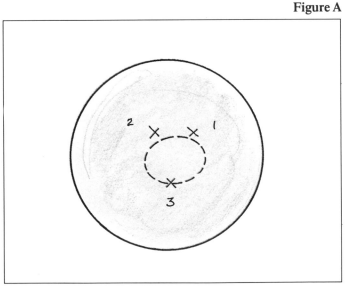

3. Continue working with the same thread to add details to the nose, following the entry and exit points that are illustrated in **Figure B**.
   - **a.** Pull the thread across the surface, enter at 4, exit at 5.
   - **b.** Pull the thread across the surface, enter at 4, exit at 6.
   - **c.** Pull the thread across the surface, enter at 4, and exit at 7. Pull the thread tightly and lock the stitch at 7.
   - **d.** Pull the thread across the surface, enter at 4, exit at 8.
   - **e.** Pull the thread across the surface, enter at 4, and exit at 9. Pull the thread tightly, and lock the stitch at 9.
   - **f.** Pull the thread across the surface, enter at 10, and exit at 11. Pull the thread gently until a lower lip appears. Lock the stitch at 11.
   - **g.** Pull the thread down across the surface, enter on the back side opposite 11, and exit at 12.
   - **h.** Pull the thread down across the surface, enter on the back side opposite 4, and exit at 4. Pull the thread

Figure B

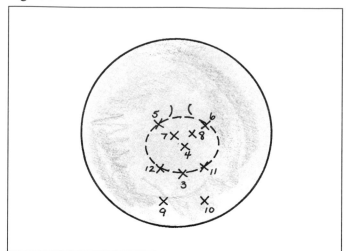

Figure C

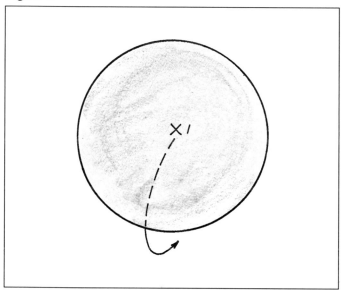

Figure D

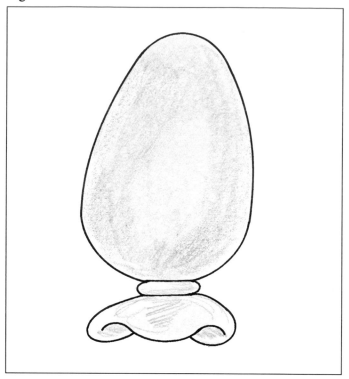

8. Gently flatten and manipulate the ball to form an elongated ear shape, as shown in **Figure D**.

9. Repeat the procedures described in steps 7 and 8 to form the second ear.

10. Repeat the procedures described in steps 7 and 8 to create the haunch portion of one hind leg, but flatten it so that the tied portion is at the bottom center of the oval shape. Make a second haunch in the same manner.

11. To make one foot, encase a ½-inch-diameter ball of fiberfill in a small piece of hose. Gather the edge, tie it off, and cut off the excess hose.

12. Follow the entry and exit points illustrated in **Figure E** to sculpt the paws on the foot.

 a. Enter at the tied portion, push the needle through the foot, and exit at 1. Pull the thread around the surface of the ball, enter at the tied portion, and exit at 1.

 b. Reenter at 1 and exit at the tied portion. Pull the thread to separate the first toe, and lock the stitch at the tie.

 c. Reenter at the tie, push the needle through the foot, and exit at 2.

 d. Pull the thread around the surface of the ball, enter at the tied portion, and exit at 2.

 e. Reenter at 2 and exit at the tie. Pull the thread to separate the toes, lock the stitch at the tie, and cut the thread.

13. Assemble three more feet, following the instructions contained in steps 11 and 12.

Assembling the Bunny

1. The assembled bunny is shown in **Figure F**. Glue the ears to the back of the head. Stitch or glue the head to the body, placing the tied side of the head against the tied side of the body;

tightly, enter at 4, and exit on the back. Pull the thread and lock the stitch. Cut the thread.

4. Glue a tiny black bead to each of the two eye depressions.

5. To make the body, cut a 5-inch-diameter circle of blue pantyhose, and wrap it around a 3-inch-diameter ball of fiberfill. Gather and tie off the edge, and trim off the excess hose.

6. To form the rabbit's posterior, follow the entry and exit points illustrated in **Figure C**. The posterior should be sculpted on the side opposite the tied portion.

 a. Enter at the tied portion, push the needle straight through the ball, and exit at 1. Pull the thread around the surface of the ball, enter directly opposite 1 at the tied portion, and exit at 1. Pull the thread tightly to form the "cheeks." Lock the stitch at 1.

 b. Reenter at 1 and exit at the tied portion. Lock the stitch and cut the thread.

7. To form one ear, cut a 2-inch-diameter circle of blue hose and wrap it around a ¾-inch-diameter ball of fiberfill. Gather the edge, tie it off, and trim off the excess hose.

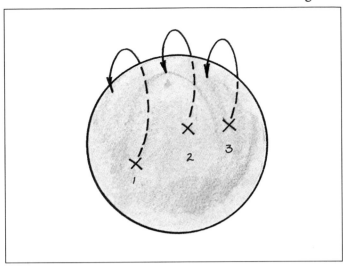

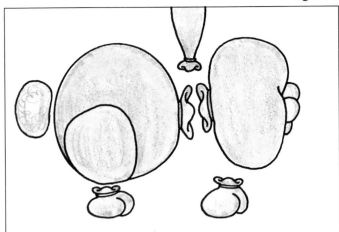

be sure that the body is rotated so that the dividing line between the "cheeks" runs in the right direction.

2. Attach two feet (these will be the front feet) to the body and head, placing the toes at the front. Attach the remaining two feet to the underside of the body just behind the two front feet, with the toes facing forward. Attach one haunch to the underside of the body, just behind and to the outside of one back foot. Attach the remaining haunch behind the other back foot.

3. Glue the light blue pompom to the bunny's back end, at the top of the sculpted dividing line, for the tail. Tie the ⅛-inch-wide lavender ribbon into a tiny bow, trim the ends at an angle, and glue it to the top of the head.

Making the Egg

1. Blow up the balloon and manipulate it to form an egg shape measuring approximately 8 inches tall. Tie the end in a knot.

2. Pull the lower leg of pink pantyhose over the balloon, so that the larger end of the egg-shaped balloon is inserted all the way to the toe end of the hose. Stretch the hose smoothly around the balloon, and tie a knot in the hose directly over the tied end of the balloon. Trim off the excess hose 1 inch above the knot.

3. Spray the entire surface of the egg with a light coating of fabric starch. Allow the starch to dry, and apply a second coat. Allow the second coat to dry, and apply a third coat.

4. When the starch is completely dry, use a razor knife to cut an oval-shaped opening in the egg, as shown in **Figure G**. This will, of course, pop the balloon. Don't worry if the egg should wrinkle slightly when the balloon pops; this probably will not happen, but if it does the egg can be smoothed out by applying a light coating of starch to the affected area, and smoothing with your fingers. When the opening is cut and removed, carefully pull away the remainder of the balloon.

5. The finished egg will sit in a stand, with the larger end of the egg at the bottom. Glue ¾-inch-wide lace around the opening that you cut into the egg, beginning and ending at the bottom of the opening. The lace should be glued to the outside of the egg, so that the scalloped edge of the lace covers the edge of the opening. Turn under the ends of the lace, overlap them slightly, and glue them in place.

6. To make a decoration for the top of the egg, cut a 4-inch square of nylon net and run a line of hand basting stitches along the center line. Pull the thread to gather the net into a fan shape, and then glue the fan to the tied portion of the hose at the top of the egg.

7. Tie the ½-inch-wide lavender satin ribbon in a bow, and glue it to the tied hose at the top of the egg. Cut the stem from each of three silk flowers, and glue the blossoms to the bow.

Final Assembly

1. The top of a spray can will serve as the base for the finished egg. Wrap the 1¾-inch lace around the circumference of the can top, overlapping the ends. Glue the lace in place. There's no need to cover the upper end of the can top, but wrap the edge of the lace around the lower edge of the top and glue it to the inside.

2. Crumple the remaining nylon net and arrange it around the inside of the egg.

3. Make a nest for the bunny in the crumpled netting, and place the bunny in his nest. Place the remaining silk flowers in the netting, arranging them as you please.

4. Place the covered base open side up on a flat surface, and place the finished egg on the stand.

Belly Up to Our Bar

Every bar needs a shady lady to set the mood, and this is definitely a shady lady! She'll fit right into your room-of-enjoyment, or give her to a friend who has a good sense of humor. The stuffed-pantyhose lady holds a fabric banner – you can reproduce our embroidered slogan on the banner or create one of your own. Overall dimensions are 22 x 28 inches.

Materials

Note: We chose a color scheme of burgundy, light blue, and fuchsia, but you may wish to choose another color combination that matches your decor.

A pair of regular-weave flesh-tone pantyhose

¼ yard of 45-inch-wide dusty-blue lightweight cotton fabric for the banner

1 yard of dusty fuchsia nylon suede cloth for the mirror frame covering fabric

6 x 11-inch rectangle of burgundy-colored velour fabric for the dress bodice

1 yard of ⅛-inch-wide burgundy satin ribbon, 1 yard of ⅛-inch-wide fuchsia grosgrain ribbon, and 1 yard of ¼-inch-wide pale blue satin ribbon

Two skeins of burgundy perle cotton embroidery thread (for the slogan), and an embroidery needle that will accommodate all six strands of thread

½ skein of burgundy acrylic knitting yarn for the hair

½ yard of bonded polyester quilt batting

A bag of polyester fiberfill

Heavy-duty brown thread and a long sharp needle

Dressmaker's carbon paper or a fabric marking pen with water-soluble ink

One set of false fingernails and fingernail polish.

6-inch length of novelty eyelashes or regular false eyelashes

One package each of pink faceted beads, pink pinwheel beads, and craft wire, for the earrings and bracelet (You can purchase costume jewelry if you prefer.)

One burgundy silk rose

One burgundy nylon neck scarf

A framed mirror with outside dimensions of 22 x 28 inches (Ours has a 2¾-inch-wide wooden frame.)

Two ½-inch-diameter wooden dowel rods, each 15 inches long

Two small screweyes and a length of picture-hanging wire

Acrylic paint in bright purple, bright blue, bright pink, white, brown, and black; and an artist's fine-tipped paintbrush

Four small and four large metal knitting needles (These will be used as forms around which the yarn will be wrapped to make it curl. If you do not have knitting needles, you can use metal rods of equivalent diameter. Whatever you use, be sure that it is oven-safe, as the yarn must be heated to retain the curl.)

Covering the Frame

1. Remove the mirror from its frame. Cut strips of bonded quilt batting to cover the frame; each strip should be about 1 inch wider and 1 inch longer than the frame member it is to cover. Glue the strips to the front of the frame, wrapping the edges of the strips around the edges of the frame.

2. Place the 1-yard length of suede cloth wrong side up on a flat surface. Place the frame right side down on top, and pull the fabric up around the outer edges of the frame. Glue the edges of the fabric to the back of the frame. To keep the fabric tight and even glue the top center first, then the bottom center, then the center of each side (**Figure A**). Continue to glue along the four edges, working toward the corners and rotating as you glue to keep the tension tight and even. Fold the corners neatly at the back, cutting away the excess fabric.

3. Mark a cutting line on the wrong side of the suede cloth, 2 inches inside each inner edge of the frame. Cut out the center portion of the fabric along each marked line, and clip the fabric from each inner corner up to the corresponding corner of the frame. Wrap the edges of the fabric around the inner edges of the frame and spot glue each one in place at the center.

4. Carefully replace the mirror inside the frame, pulling the free inner edges of the fabric to smooth the fabric on the front of the frame.

Making the Shady Lady

The shady lady's chest and arms are shaped from a single stuffed pantyhose leg, as shown in **Figure B**.

1. Cut one leg from the pantyhose at the panty line. Stuff one-third of the leg, at the toe end, until it is about 7 inches in circumference and 17 inches long; this will be one arm. Stuff the

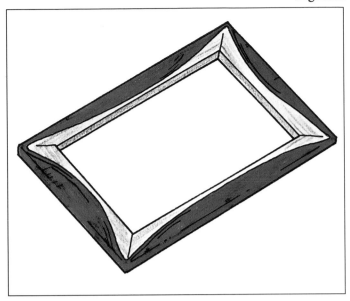

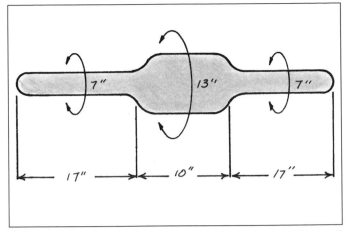

Figure C

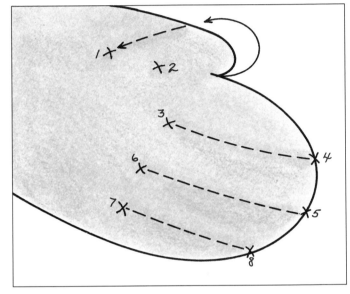

middle third until it is approximately 13 inches in circumference and 10 inches long; this will be the chest. Stuff the remaining third of the pantyhose until it is about 7 inches in circumference and 17 inches long; this will be the second arm. Manipulate the fiberfill until the arms are evenly shaped. Tie off the open end of the hose, using thread, and cut off the excess.

2. Each end of the stuffed hose is sculpted to form a hand. Use a long sharp needle and heavy-duty brown thread, and follow the entry and exit points illustrated in **Figure C**. Begin by sculpting the toe end of the hose.

    a. Insert the needle on the underside (the palm side of the hand), 5 inches from the end of the hand. Push the needle straight through the hand and exit on the back. This will be the base of the thumb.

    b. Pinch up a ridge on the thumb side of the hand. Enter at 2 and exit directly opposite 2 on the palm.

    c. Wrap the thread around the end of the hand, enter at 2 on the back, and exit at 1 on the palm.

    d. Pull the thread to separate the thumb, and lock the stitch. Reenter at 1 and exit at 3 on the back.

    e. Stitch up and down through the hand along the dotted line between points 3 and 4, exiting at 4.

    f. Reenter at 4 and exit at 5. Pull the thread and lock the stitch at 5.

    g. To form the remaining three fingers repeat the same procedures, stitching between 5 and 6, and then between 7 and 8.

    h. Lock the last stitch and cut the thread.

3. Repeat the procedures described in step 2 to sculpt the hand at the opposite end of the stuffed hose, reversing the position of the thumb. Before you begin sculpting, manipulate the hose so the tied portion is on the palm side, about halfway between the end of the hand and the area that will become the base of the fingers. The knot and excess hose will be hidden from view when the lady is attached to the mirror.

4. Paint the false fingernails and glue them to the fingers.

5. To create the shady lady's ample bust, insert the needle into the back of the chest area, at about the center. Push the needle straight through the chest and exit at the center front. Wrap the thread downward around the circumference of the chest, on the outside of the hose, and take a small stitch at the center back. Pull the thread gently to divide the breasts until the desired amount of fullness is achieved. Lock the stitch at the center back and cut the thread.

6. To make the dress bodice, press a ½-inch-wide hem to the wrong side of the fabric along each edge of the 6 x 11-inch burgundy velour rectangle. Hand stitch the hem.

7. Place the hemmed bodice against the lower portion of the shady lady's bust area, and adjust the upper long edge to reveal an ample amount of "decolletage." Secure each upper corner of the bodice by stitching through the stuffed body. Lock each stitch on the back. The lower corners will be secured later.

Making the Head

1. To form the head, tie a knot at the panty line of the remaining leg of pantyhose. Cut off the panty 1 inch above the knot, and cut across the leg 14 inches below the knot. Turn the hose so the knot is on the inside.

Figure D

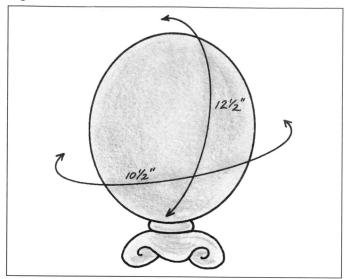

Figure F

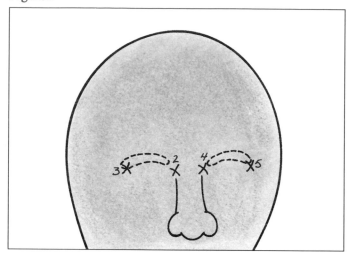

Figure E

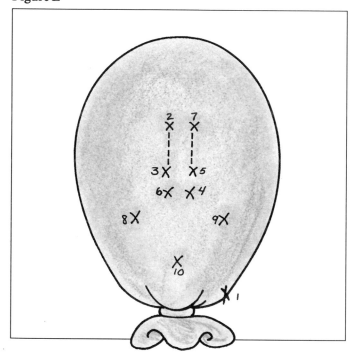

2. Stuff generous amounts of fiberfill inside the hose, manipulating the shape until a head is formed. The front two-thirds of the head should be filled out normally but the back of the head should be flat, as it will rest flat against the mirror. The head should measure 12½ inches from top to bottom around the outside of the front, and 10½ inches from side to side around the front (**Figure D**). Tie off the bottom of the hose, using thread or string, and cut off the excess hose below the tie.

3. To sculpt the nose, use a long sharp needle and heavy-duty thread. Follow the entry and exit points illustrated in **Figure E**.

    a. Enter at 1 and exit at 2. Pinch up a vertical ridge in the center of the face, and stitch back and forth under the ridge, exiting at 3. The lower end of the nose should be a bit wider than the upper end.

    b. Pull the thread gently and lock the stitch at 3.

    c. To form the nostrils, reenter at 3 and exit at 4.

    d. Reenter ¼ inch above 4 and exit at 3.

    e. Reenter at 3 and exit at 5.

    f. Reenter at 5 and exit at 6.

    g. Reenter ¼ inch above 6 and exit at 7. Pull the thread and lock the stitch under the bridge of the nose, exiting at 7. Do not cut the thread.

4. Continue working with the same thread to form the mouth, still following the entry and exit points illustrated in **Figure E**.

    a. Reenter at 7 and exit at 8.

    b. Pull the thread across the surface, enter at 9, and exit at point 3.

    c. Pull the thread until a smile appears. Lock the stitch at 3, reenter at 3, and exit at 10.

    d. Reenter at 10 and exit at 3. Pull the thread until a chin dimple appears, and lock the stitch at 3. Reenter at 3 and exit at 1.

    e. Lock the stitch and cut the thread.

5. To form the eyes and eyelids, follow the entry and exit points illustrated in **Figure F**.

    a. Enter at 1 and exit at 2.

    b. Pull the thread across the surface, enter at 3, and exit at 2. Pull the thread gently until the left eye line appears and lock the stitch at 2.

    c. Pinch up a narrow, curved ridge over the left eye, to create the eyelid.

    d. Reenter at 2 and stitch back and forth under the ridge, exiting at 3.

    e. Reenter at 3 and exit at 2. Pull the thread and lock the stitch at 2.

    f. Reenter at 2 and exit at 4.

6. Repeat the procedures described in step 5 to form the eye and eyelid on the right side of the face. Lock the stitch at the final exit point and cut the thread.

7. Paint the eyes, using acrylic paint and a small paintbrush. First, paint the entire eye socket using white paint. Allow the paint to dry completely, and then paint a blue iris in the center of each eye. When the blue paint has dried, paint a small black pupil in the center of each eye.

Figure H

8. Paint a large bright pink spot on each cheek, and paint the lips in the same grotesque color. Use a garish purple color to paint eyeshadow above each eyelid, and paint a brown eyebrow above each eye. Use black or gray to paint the lower eyelashes below each eye line. Glue false eyelashes to each eyelid.

Curling the Hair

The hair is made by wrapping acrylic yarn around large and small knitting needles, wetting the yarn, and then drying it in an oven to preserve the curls.

1. Preheat your oven to 150 degrees (warm oven).

2. Wrap knitting yarn tightly around each of the four small and four large knitting needles. Tie the ends securely.

3. Thoroughly wet each of the yarn-covered needles and place them in the oven until dry (this should take about two hours). The hair will be attached to the head later.

Making the Banner

1. Fold the rectangle of dusty blue cotton fabric in half lengthwise, placing right sides together. Stitch a 1-inch-wide seam along the aligned long raw edges, leaving the ends open.

2. Turn the stitched tube right side out, adjust it so that the seam runs along the center of one side, and press. Cut a 4 x 36-inch strip of bonded quilt batting and insert the strip inside the tube. Adjust the batting so that it is at the center of the fabric, leaving an equal amount of unstuffed fabric at each end.

3. A scale drawing of the "Belly up to our Bar" slogan is provided in **Figure G**. Enlarge the drawing to make a full-size pattern on dressmaker's pattern paper or on tracing paper. (If you prefer, create your own slogan and make a full-size pattern. The letters should be no more than 3 inches from top to bottom, and the slogan should be no longer than 26 inches.)

4. Pin the pattern to the banner, centering the slogan on the side of the fabric that does not include the seam (**Figure H**).

Transfer the slogan to the fabric, using dressmaker's carbon paper or a water-soluble fabric marking pen.

5. To embroider the message, work a backstitch along the outlines of all of the letters, using the embroidery needle threaded with all six strands of burgundy embroidery thread. (See Tips & Techniques, if necessary, for instructions on working the backstitch.) When you have completed the embroidery, press the banner gently on the wrong side using a steam iron.

6. Cut a wedge-shaped piece from each end of the banner, turn the raw edges to the inside, and whipstitch them together, as shown in **Figure I**.

Final Assembly

We suggest that you arrange all of the elements on top of the mirror while the mirror is lying flat. When the arrangement is to your liking, glue the elements in place. Our arrangement is shown in **Figure J**.

1. If you purchased costume jewelry, skip this step and proceed to step 2. To make the shady lady's earrings, cut a 6-inch length of craft wire. Thread a bead onto the wire and wrap one end of the wire around the bead to secure it. Thread additional beads onto the wire, leaving 2 inches of wire at the opposite end. Cut two additional 6-inch lengths of wire and thread each length with beads in the same manner. Wrap the free ends of the three beaded wires together. Thread a few beads onto the wrapped

Figure I

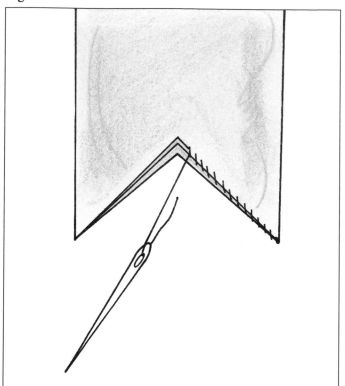

Figure J

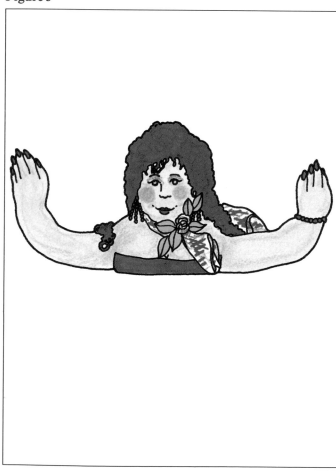

Figure K

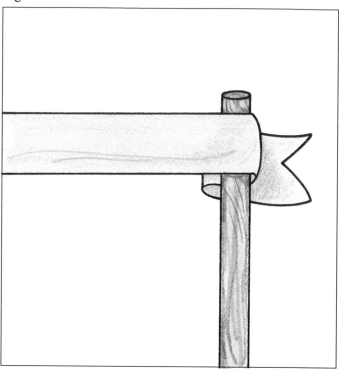

ends of wire, and secure with glue. Make a second earring in the same manner. To create a bracelet, cut a length of craft wire about 3 inches longer than a measurement taken around the shady lady's wrist. Thread beads onto the wire and twist the ends together.

2. Place the sculpted chest at the center of the lower member of the frame, and position the head directly above the chest. Glue the head to the chest. Wrap the scarf around the neck and tie it in a knot at one side. Glue the silk rose to the knotted scarf. Glue the lower edge of the dress bodice to the frame bottom.

3. Arrange one arm so that it extends along the lower frame member and turns upward at the corner of the frame. Arrange the other arm in the same manner. Turn the hands so that the palm sides face the frame, and slip the bracelet around one wrist. Glue one end of a dowel rod into each hand. Place the banner along the upper frame member, over the upper end of each dowel rod. Tuck the banner under each dowel rod, as shown in **Figure K**.

4. Remove the curled yarn from the smaller knitting needles; the yarn should remain tightly curled. Cut the yarn into short lengths and glue them to the head to form the bangs.

5. When you remove the yarn from the larger knitting needles the curls probably will tend to loosen. Carefully slide the yarn off of each needle, cut it into shorter lengths, and glue them to the head.

6. When everything is arranged correctly (**Figure L**), glue all of the elements in place. Glue or tack an earring to each side of the head. Wrap all three ribbons around the top of one dowel rod and tie them together in a bow, allowing the ends to hang freely. Trim both ends of each ribbon at an angle.

7. Insert a small screweye into the back of each vertical frame member and attach the hanging wire between them.

Materials

For the fabric insert:

18 x 21-inch rectangle of calico fabric for the background

One leg of nurse's white pantyhose

A small amount of polyester fiberfill

5-inch length of 3½-inch-wide white eyelet trim

12-inch length of ½-inch-wide white lace trim or ribbon

12-inch length of ½-inch-wide deep yellow grosgrain ribbon

Remnant of gold-colored cotton fabric for the feet and beaks

Two ⅜-inch-diameter flat black buttons for the eyes

Water-soluble fabric marking pen

Regular white thread

For the wooden frame:

14 linear feet of oak or pine 1 x 4

3-foot length of ¾-inch-diameter wooden dowel rod

Twenty No. 6 gauge flathead wood screws, each 1 inch long

Carpenter's wood glue, or hot-melt glue and a glue gun

Cutting the Fabrics

1. Scale drawings for the Goose and Gander Body patterns are provided in **Figure A**. Enlarge the drawings to make full-size patterns, and transfer the dotted wing detail lines to the Gander Body pattern.

2. Full-size patterns for the Goose Beak, Gander Beak, and Foot are provided in **Figure B**. Trace the patterns onto tracing or pattern paper.

3. Cut one Goose Beak, one Gander Beak, and four Foot pieces from gold-colored cotton fabric.

4. Cut off the pantyhose leg at the panty line, and then cut off the toe, to form a tube. Cut open the leg tube lengthwise and place it on a flat surface.

5. Place the full-size Body patterns on top of the single layer of hose, allowing a margin of at least 1 inch around the outer edge of each pattern. Trace around the outer edge of each pattern, using the water-soluble pen. When you cut the Body pieces, cut along the margin line 1 inch outside the traced outline, not along the traced outline itself. The margins will be cut away after you have appliqued the pieces to the backing fabric.

Assembling the Insert

1. Arrange the Body and Beak pieces on the right side of the background fabric, as shown in **Figure C**, and pin them in place. Use a closely spaced zigzag setting to machine stitch around each Body piece along the traced outline, and around the outer edge of each Beak. The applique stitching should cover the edges of the Beak pieces.

2. Carefully stretch the hose margins and trim the excess as close to the applique stitches as you can.

3. The geese are stuffed through small slits cut into the backing fabric. Turn the assembly wrong side up and slit the backing fabric at the center of each body, being careful not to slit the hose as well. Stuff fiberfill through each opening until the front is as plump as you like; you can use the blunt end of a knitting needle or other such object to push the fiberfill into the more

Goose & Gander Hat Rack

Here's a project that's fair for the goose and the gander! Any crafty soul with a gaggle of coats and hats cluttering up the closet can create this wooden frame and decorative fabric insert. Overall size is 24 x 30 inches.

remote parts of the bodies. When the geese are stuffed sufficiently, whipstitch the slits closed.

4. Turn the assembly right side up and use a straight hand or machine stitch to create the wing details on the gander, following the dotted lines on the pattern. The stitches should pass through the hose, the stuffing, and the backing fabric.

5. To create an eye for the gander, sew a button to his head, as shown in **Figure D**. The button stitches should pass through all thicknesses, and the thread should be pulled to create a slight indentation around the button. Stitch a button eye to the goose's face as well.

6. To assemble one foot, place two Foot pieces right sides together and stitch a narrow seam along the contoured edges, leaving the short straight end open, as shown in **Figure E**. Clip the corners and turn the foot right side out. Assemble the two remaining Foot pieces in the same manner.

7. To join the two feet, stack one on top of the other and stitch along the open edges. Press the seam open. To attach the feet to the gander, fold them open along the seam that joins them

1 square = 1 inch

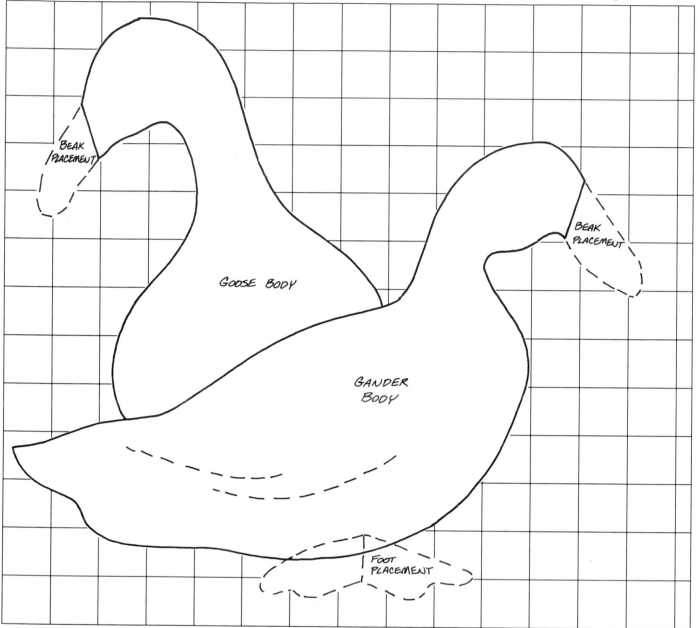

BEAK
PLACEMENT

GOOSE BODY

BEAK
PLACEMENT

GANDER
BODY

FOOT
PLACEMENT

Figure B

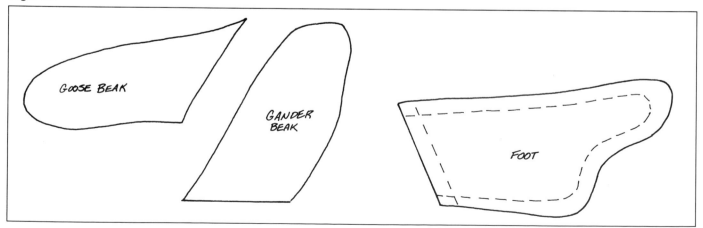

GOOSE BEAK

GANDER
BEAK

FOOT

Figure C

Figure E

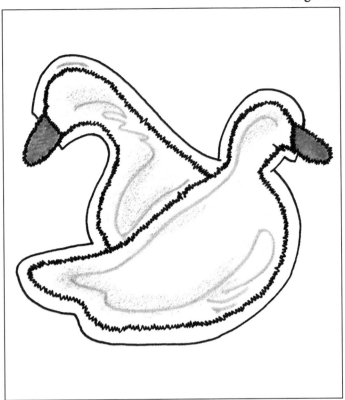

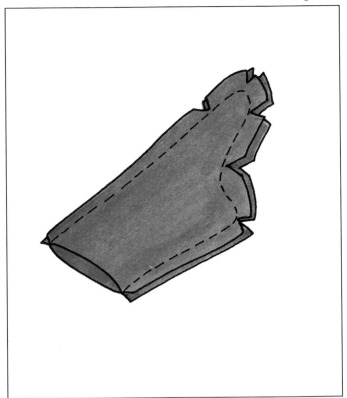

and glue them to the backing fabric so that they overlap the applique stitches at the lower edge of the gander (**Figure F**).

8. To make the goose's bonnet, turn a narrow hem to the wrong side of the eyelet trim along the bound edge and along each end. Glue the hem allowance to the goose's head, as shown in **Figure G**. Tie the narrow lace trim into a bow, and glue it to the goose's neck just below the bonnet.

9. The gander sports a dashing bow. Tie the yellow grosgrain ribbon into a bow, and glue it to the gander's neck.

GOOSE & GANDER HAT RACK

Figure G

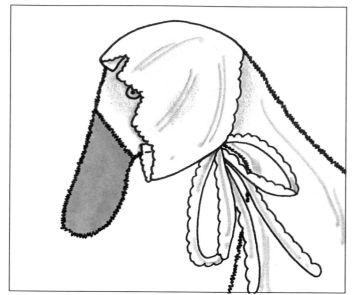

Figure H

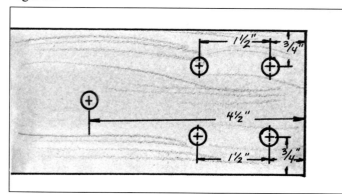

Figure I

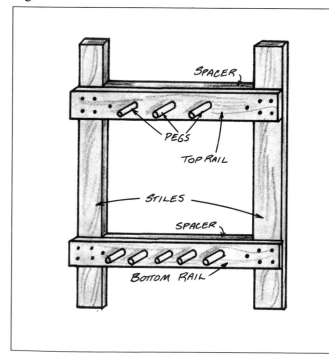

SPACER

PEGS

TOP RAIL

STILES

SPACER

BOTTOM RAIL

Assembling the Frame

1. A simple wooden assembly supports eight dowel-rod pegs and provides a frame for the fabric insert. For the frame, cut from 1 x 4 two 24-inch Rails, two 30-inch Stiles, and two 17-inch Spacers.

2. Cut eight 4-inch Pegs from ¾-inch-diameter wooden dowel rod. Round off one end of each Peg, and cut the opposite end at a slight angle. You'll also need twenty-two wooden plugs to cover the screw heads; each plug should be ½ inch in diameter and about ¼ inch thick. You can cut the plugs from leftover pine or oak using a plug cutter, or you can simply cut ¼-inch lengths of ½-inch-diameter wooden dowel rod to serve as plugs.

3. Drill five ½-inch-diameter sockets, ½ inch deep, near one end of a Rail, as shown in **Figure H**. Drill a ⅛-inch-diameter hole through the center of each socket, as shown. Drill the Rail near the opposite end in the same manner. Drill the remaining Rail in the same manner. For the pegs, drill three ¾-inch-diameter holes through one Rail (this will be the top Rail), centered between the edges, at 8-, 12-, and 16-inch intervals from one end, as shown in **Figure I**. The holes should be drilled at a slight angle toward the lower edge of the Rail, so your hats won't fall off the pegs. Drill the same size holes at an angle through the bottom Rail at 6-, 9-, 12-, 15-, and 18-inch intervals.

4. The assembled frame is shown in **Figure I**. To begin, place the two Stiles about 17 inches apart on a flat work surface. Place one of the Spacers between the Stiles, 5 inches below the aligned upper ends. Place the second Spacer between the Stiles, 5 inches above the aligned lower ends. Press the Stiles inward so they are flush against the ends of the Spacers, and glue the ends of the Spacers to the Stiles.

5. Place the top Rail across the Stiles 5 inches below the upper ends, as shown, so that it is aligned with the Spacer underneath it. Be sure that the Rail is turned so that the peg holes angle downward toward the lower edge of the Rail. Insert a screw through each of the four end holes into the Stile below, at each end of the Rail. Install the bottom Rail in the same manner, 5 inches above the lower ends of the Stiles.

6. To secure the upper Spacer, insert a screw through each remaining end hole of the top Rail, into the Spacer. Secure the lower Spacer in the same manner. Insert and glue a wooden plug into each socket to cover the screw heads.

7. Insert a liberal amount of glue into one of the Peg holes in the top Rail. Insert the angled end of a Peg into the glued hole, turning it so that the outer rounded end angles upward. Glue a Peg into each remaining hole in the same manner.

8. Sand and stain the frame, or finish by simply rubbing vegetable oil into it.

9. To install the hat rack on the wall, we drilled a ½-inch-diameter socket ½-inch deep through each stile near the upper end. After you've screwed the rack to the wall, cover the screw heads with ½-inch-diameter wooden plugs.

Final Assembly

To install the fabric insert, run a bead of glue around the back of the frame opening. If you're using hot-melt glue, carefully position the insert and press it down against the top spacer only, then stretch the fabric slightly as you press the sides and lower edge to the frame. If you're using white glue, tack the insert to the back of the frame and stretch it before you apply the glue.

Materials

18-inch-diameter grapevine wreath (If you wish to make your own wreath, you'll need generous amounts of grapevines, wisteria, or other long, flexible green vines; a roll of string; and a cylindrical object about 11 inches in diameter, such as a small wastepaper basket, that will serve as the form when you weave the wreath.)

One bunch of dried baby's-breath

5-yard length of 1¼-inch-wide decorative ribbon (We used burgundy-colored calico ribbon with lace edging.)

For the sheep:

5 x 5-inch-square of off-white acrylic fleece

Scrap of black vinyl or felt for the ears

7-inch length of ¼-inch-wide velvet ribbon (We used burgundy-colored ribbon.)

A small amount of polyester fiberfill

¼ x 1 x 4-inch piece of scrap wood for the base

One round-top craft clothespin

Four 1½-inch lengths of ¼-inch-diameter wooden dowel rod for the legs

One tiny gold bell

Black paint

White glue or hot-melt glue and a glue gun

For Bo Peep:

8-inch length of regular-weave flesh-tone pantyhose

1 yard of 2-inch-wide ivory-colored gathered eyelet trim

¼ yard of unbleached muslin or ivory-colored cotton fabric

7-inch length of ½-inch-wide velvet ribbon for the staff (We used burgundy.)

5-inch length of ⅛-inch-wide velvet ribbon for the hair ties

A small amount of yarn for the hair

A small amount of polyester fiberfill

Heavy-duty flesh-tone thread; a long sharp needle; and thread to match the fabric

2½ x 6-inch polystyrene foam or cardboard cone

One wire coat hanger or an 18-inch length of craft wire

Cosmetic cheek blusher

Felt-tip markers in red and black

Making the Wreath

1. If you purchased a wreath, skip this section and proceed to the next section, "Decorating the Wreath." To begin making your grapevine wreath, choose one long vine and wrap it around the cylindrical object you have selected for the form. Secure the ends of the vine by twisting them around each other.

2. Weave a second vine over and under the first one, and twist the ends together.

3. Continue to weave additional vines around the form, passing over, under, and through the first two. Begin weaving at a different spot each time, so that the twisted ends are not all at the same place. It may be necessary to hold some of the previous vines in place as you weave more and more vines around the form. Continue to add vines until your wreath is about 18 inches in diameter, and looks full.

4. Carefully remove the wreath from the form and tie lengths of string around the wreath to secure it while it dries.

Bo Peep Wreath

Little Bo Peep has found her lost sheep hiding in this beautiful grapevine wreath. Wrapped in ribbons and topped with a full bow, this wreath adds just the right touch to your home decor. It measures 18 inches in diameter.

It may take two or three days for the vines to dry completely. Once the wreath has dried, you can either remove the strings or leave them in place and cover them with ribbon when you decorate the wreath.

Decorating the Wreath

1. Begin by wrapping the decorative ribbon around the wreath, as shown in **Figure A**, beginning about 12 inches from the end of the ribbon so the end can hang freely. Leave spaces between the successive wraps of ribbon, as shown. When you reach the starting point again, cut off the ribbon, leaving another 12-inch length to hang freely. Cut the ends of the ribbon at an angle and tie them together in a knot at the start/stop point.

2. To make the bow, wrap the remaining ribbon into a continuous loop, approximately 8 inches in diameter. Fold the wrapped loop of ribbon in half and clip the fold on each side, as shown in **Figure B**. Be careful not to cut the ribbon in half. Tie the ribbon securely at the cut marks using a piece of string.

3. Twist, pull, and turn out each loop of ribbon, one at a time, until a full bow is formed.

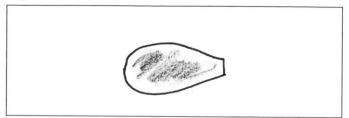

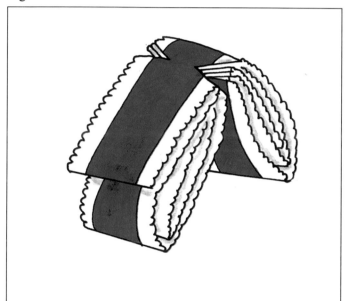

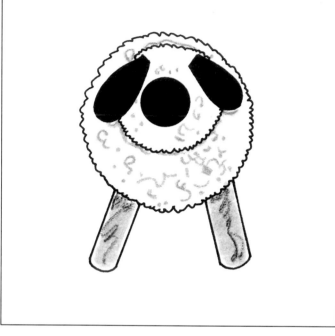

4. Place the bow on the wreath, on top of the wrapped-ribbon knot, and secure it using glue or whipstitches.

5. Arrange sprigs of the dried baby's-breath around the front of the wreath, inserting the stems underneath the wraps of ribbon. When you have an arrangement you like, glue the baby's-breath in place.

Making the Sheep

1. Glue the dowel-rod legs to the clothespin, positioning them so they are at a slight angle, as shown in **Figure C**. This assembly will serve as the sheep's body.

2. Center the body assembly on one side of the scrap-wood base, and glue the legs in place.

3. Paint the base, legs, and clothespin black. Allow the paint to dry thoroughly.

4. Round off the corners of the 5 x 5-inch-square of acrylic fleece. Place a small amount of fiberfill in the center of the fleece, and wrap it around the clothespin. Adjust the amount of fiberfill, if necessary, so the sheep looks plump.

5. The head of the clothespin will be the sheep's nose. Adjust the fleece and glue the front edge to the circumference edge of the clothespin head. Wrap the side edges of the fleece to the underside of the sheep, and glue them to the legs and to each other underneath the sheep body, trimming and tucking where necessary. Fold and glue the back edge of the fleece so that it covers the opposite end of the clothespin body.

Figure C

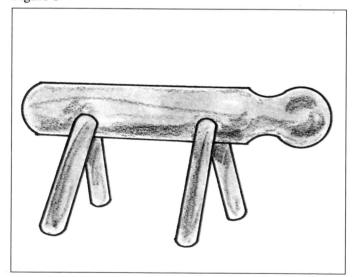

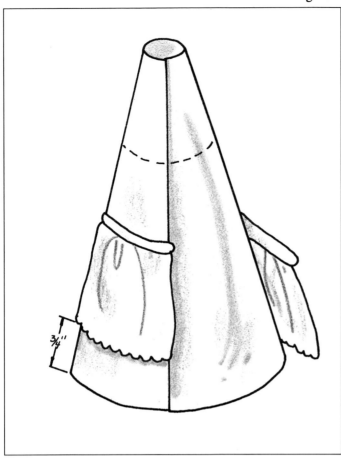

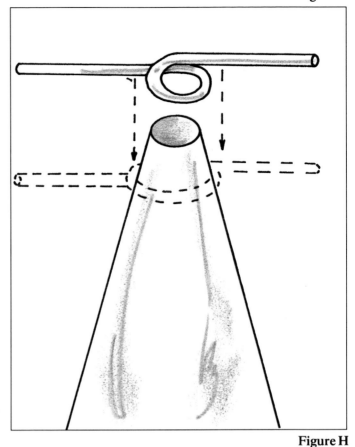

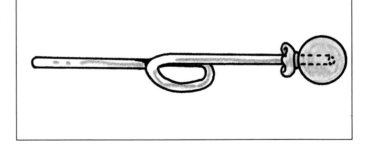

6. A full-size pattern for the Ear is provided in **Figure D**. Cut two Ears from the scrap of black vinyl or felt. Glue them to the top of the sheep's head, as shown in **Figure E**.

7. Thread the ribbon through the bell hanger and slide the bell to the center of the ribbon. Wrap the ribbon around the sheep's neck and tie it in a bow at the top.

Assembling Bo Peep

1. The cardboard or foam cone will serve as Bo Peep's body, and it will be covered with fabric and eyelet to create the dress. Cut off the topmost ¼ inch of the cone tip.

2. To cover the cone with the muslin or cotton fabric, lay the cone on its side along one edge of the fabric and glue this edge of the fabric to the cone. Roll the cone along the fabric until the attached fabric edge meets the fabric again. Glue or pin the edges of the fabric together. Trim the excess fabric from the cone, leaving enough at the large open end so that you can turn it under to form a hem. Turn the hem under (but not around the lower edge of the cone), and glue or stitch it.

3. Bo Peep's dress consists of layers of eyelet trim wrapped around the fabric-covered cone. To wrap the first layer, place one end of the trim at the back of the cone (where the fabric edges meet) so that the lower edge of the trim is about ¾ inch above the lower hemmed edge of the muslin, as shown in **Figure F**. Wrap the trim around the cone until the ends overlap at the back. Cut off the excess eyelet, and glue the ends together.

4. Wrap another layer of eyelet trim around the cone, so that the lower edge of the trim covers the upper edge of the first layer. Secure this layer in the same manner as you did the first. The arms and head are attached before the last layer of eyelet trim is added.

Making the Arms

1. Cut an 8-inch length of craft wire or clothes hanger, and bend it into a loop at the center, as shown in **Figure G**.

2. To make one little round hand, place a small amount (approximately ½ inch) of fiberfill around one end of the wire. Wrap a small circle of pantyhose around the fiberfill, and tie the edge to the wire using thread (**Figure H**). Follow the same procedures to create a hand at the opposite end of the wire.

3. Cut a piece of muslin or cotton fabric that is approximately 2½ x 4 inches for one sleeve.

Figure I

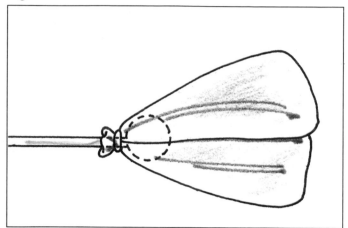

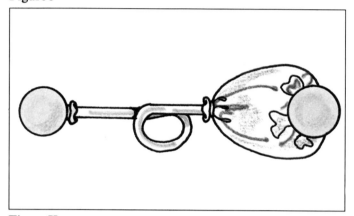

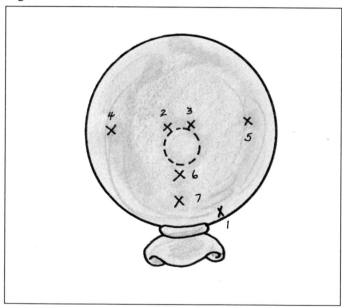

Figure L

4. Place the Sleeve piece right side up on a flat surface. Place one of the hands on top of the Sleeve, as shown in **Figure I**, so that it is centered between the long edges and extends about ½ inch over the end. Gather the fabric around the wire just behind the fist, and secure it tightly with several wraps of thread.

5. Fold the Sleeve back over the wire arm, and secure the opposite end of the Sleeve to the wire near the loop with several tight wraps of thread (**Figure J**). Glue the long edges together.

6. Repeat the procedures described in steps 3 through 5 to create the other sleeve.

7. Bend the wire arms toward each other. Slip the wire loop over the top of the cone, so that the arms face front, and glue or tack it in place.

Making the Head

1. Wrap a 3-inch-diameter circle of pantyhose around a 1½-inch-diameter ball of fiberfill. Gather and tie the edge of the hose using thread.

2. To soft-sculpt the facial features, use heavy-duty flesh-tone thread and a long sharp needle. Follow the entry and exit points illustrated in **Figure K**.

    a. Enter at 1 where the hose is tied, push the needle through the head, and exit at 2.

    b. To form the nose, sew a tiny circle of small running stitches, and exit at 3.

    c. Use the tip of the needle to gently lift the fiberfill within the circle. Gently pull the thread until a little round nose appears. Lock the stitch and exit at 2.

    d. To form the eyes, pull the thread across the surface, enter at 4, and exit at 3.

    e. Pull the thread across the surface, enter at 5, and exit at 2. Gently pull the thread until the eye lines appear. Lock the stitch at 2.

    f. To form the mouth, reenter at 2 and exit at 6. Reenter slightly to one side of 6 and exit at 3. Pull the thread until the top lip forms.

    g. Reenter at 3 and exit at 7. Reenter slightly to the side of 7 and exit at 2. Pull the thread until the lower lip appears. Lock the stitch at 2. Reenter at 2, exit at 1, lock the stitch, and cut the thread.

3. To make the hair, cut six 8-inch lengths of yarn and tie the strands together at the center using thread. Position the tied center of the yarn on the top of the head, and glue or whipstitch it in place.

4. On one side of the head, separate the yarn into three double strands. Begin braiding the strands at what would be the bottom of the ear, and continue braiding until there is approximately ½ inch remaining. Tie the end of the braid, using one-half of the ⅛-inch-wide ribbon (**Figure L**).

5. Repeat the procedures described in step 4 to braid the yarn on the opposite side of the head.

6. Place the head on the body, inserting the knot into the cut-out tip of the cone. Glue or whipstitch the head in place.

7. Add a little color to the cheeks, using the cosmetic blusher. Use the red felt-tip marker to color her lips, and the black felt-tip marker to make two small dots for the eyes.

8. The final layer of eyelet trim will hide the neck stitches, the exposed wire loop, and the gathered tops of the sleeves. Wrap the eyelet around the neck, and secure it at the back in the same manner as you did the others.

9. To make the bonnet, cut a 3 x 7-inch rectangle of muslin or cotton fabric. Fold the rectangle in half lengthwise, placing wrong sides together, and run a line of basting stitches through both layers of fabric, close to the aligned long raw edges; do not cut off the tails of thread.

10. Cut a 1⅜ x 6-inch rectangle of muslin or cotton fabric for the bonnet Binding. Place the Binding piece right side up on a flat surface, and place the basted Bonnet piece on top, aligning the basted edge of the Bonnet with one long edge of the Binding. Pull up the basting threads to gather the Bonnet evenly so it matches the length of the Binding. Tie off the gathering threads and stitch the Bonnet to the Binding, ¼ inch from the aligned edges. Turn the Binding upward and press the seam allowances toward the Binding.

11. Press a ¼-inch allowance to the wrong side of the fabric along the free long edge of the Binding piece. Fold the Binding piece in half lengthwise, placing wrong sides together, so that it encases the gathered edge of the Bonnet, and whipstitch the pressed edge to the Bonnet. The ends of the assembled bonnet can remain unfinished, or you can hem them if you like.

12. Place the bonnet on Bo Peep's head; the binding goes at the back, and the folded edge of the bonnet goes at the front. The front edge of the bonnet should extend out over the face, and the ends should be placed behind the shoulders. When you have the bonnet arranged to your liking, glue it to the head.

Final Assembly

1. To make Bo Peep's staff, cut an 8-inch length of craft wire or clothes hanger, and bend one end to form a hook. Wrap the ½-inch-wide ribbon around the staff near the hook, and tie the ends in a bow. Glue the ribbon to the staff.

2. The assembled wreath is shown in **Figure M**. Place Bo Peep on the inside rim of the wreath, just to one side of the bottom center point. The bow should be at the top of the wreath, with the free ends of ribbon hanging downward. Glue the base of Bo Peep's body cone to the wreath.

3. Place the hook of the staff over Bo Peep's arm and glue the lower end to the wreath.

4. To attach the sheep to the wreath, create a small opening on one side of the wreath by spreading apart some of the grapevines wide enough to insert the back of the base. Glue the base to the wreath.

Portia and Skipper

Just for kicks, we made these adorable twins from tube socks. They're great for a kid who's tough on dolls, but soft on dollmakers. Each doll measures approximately 24 inches tall.

Materials

Two pairs of off-white 20-inch heavy tube socks, each with a 3-inch solid-color ribbed top

½ yard of blue gingham for Portia's dress

⅛ yard of white cotton knit T-shirt fabric for Skipper's shirt

¼ yard of blue denim fabric for the knickers and shoes

2¼ yards of 1-inch-wide white eyelet trim

1 yard of 1-inch-wide blue satin ribbon for Portia's pigtails

⅛ yard of blue ribbing for Skipper's shirt

1 yard of ⅛-inch-wide elastic

One hook and eye closure

Four blue ⅜-inch-diameter shank-type buttons for the eyes

One skein of orange rug yarn for the hair

A bag of polyester fiberfill

Heavy-duty white thread; a long sharp needle; and regular thread to match the fabrics

White glue or hot-melt glue and a glue gun

Cosmetic cheek blusher

Brown eyebrow pencil

Black felt-tip marking pen

Cutting the Pieces

1. Scale drawings for the Shirt, Knickers, Sleeve, Shoe, Dress Back, and Dress Front are provided in **Figure A**. Enlarge the scale drawings to make full-size patterns. Be sure to transfer the placement circles and all other sewing directions to the full-size patterns.

2. Cut the pattern pieces from the fabrics as listed below:

Blue gingham: Dress Front – cut one
                Dress Back – cut two
                Sleeve – cut two
Denim: Shoe – cut four
       Knickers – cut two
White cotton T-shirt knit: Shirt – cut two

Making the Bodies

Note: Portia and Skipper are made identically except for their hair. Use one pair of tube socks for each doll. All seam allowances are ¼-inch-wide unless otherwise noted.

1. To make the torso, cut off the ribbed section of one sock. This will be the only unused part. Stuff the remaining portion of the sock firmly with polyester fiberfill until the toe end is about 13 inches in circumference.

2. To form the head, wrap a length of heavy-duty thread several times around the stuffed sock, approximately 6 inches from the closed end (**Figure B**). Tie off the thread.

3. The portion of the sock below the tied head will be the torso. It should be stuffed to within ½ inch of the open end, and should be about 11 inches in circumference.

4. Cut the second sock in half crosswise (**Figure C**). The arms will be made from the toe half. Cut this section in half lengthwise (**Figure D**). Fold one Arm piece in half lengthwise, placing right sides together. Stitch the seam along the long straight edge, leaving the short straight end open and unstitched (**Figure D**). Turn the arm right side out, stuff it with fiberfill, and stitch the open edges together. The arm should be about 4 inches in circumference. Make another arm in the same manner, using the other half of the toe portion.

5. Tie off the hand about 2 inches from the curved end of the arm, using heavy-duty thread (**Figure E**). To create the elbow, either tie it off 2 inches above the wrist as you did the hand and head, or take two stitches back and forth through the arm at that point, pull the thread until an indentation appears, lock the stitch, and cut the thread.

6. To soft-sculpt the fingers, use heavy-duty thread and a long sharp needle, and follow the entry and exit points illustrated in **Figure F**.
    a. Enter the needle at point 1 (on the wrist), and exit at 2 (on what will be the back of the hand).
    b. Slightly flatten the ball of fiberfill at the end to form the finger portion of the hand. Wrap the thread around the end of the hand, enter on the front of the hand directly opposite point 2, and exit at 2. Pull the thread tightly to form the first finger.
    c. To begin the next finger, reenter at 2 and exit at 3.
    d. Wrap the thread around the end of the hand, enter on the front side directly opposite point 3, and then exit at point 3 on the back. Pull the thread tightly to form the second finger.

1 square = 1 inch

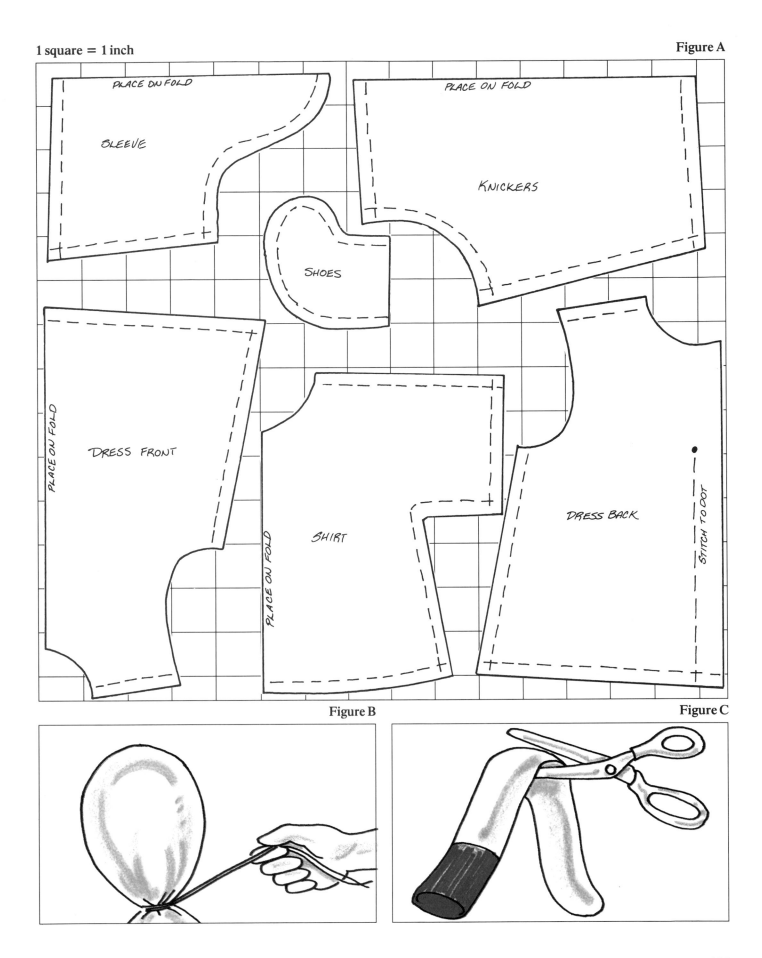

PLACE ON FOLD

SLEEVE

PLACE ON FOLD

KNICKERS

SHOES

PLACE ON FOLD

DRESS FRONT

PLACE ON FOLD

SHIRT

DRESS BACK

STITCH TO DOT

Figure B

Figure C

Figure D

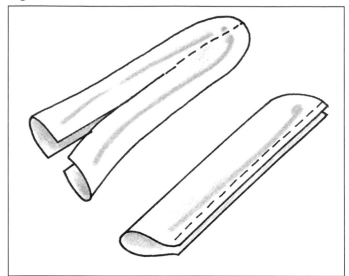

Figure E

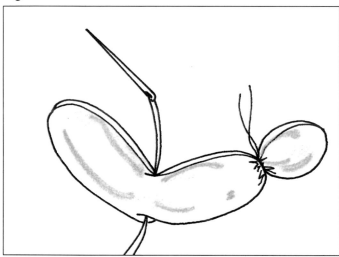

Figure F

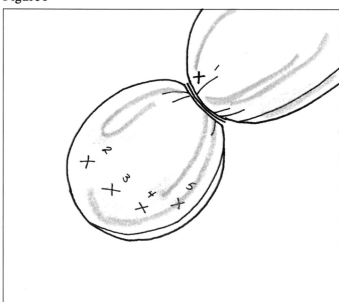

Figure G

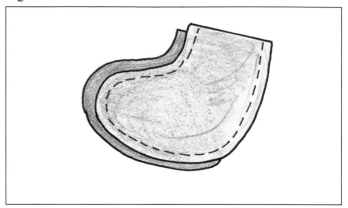

Figure H

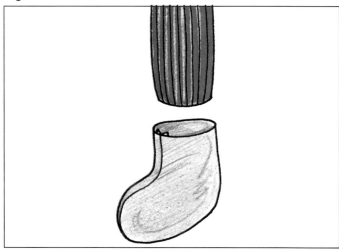

    e. Repeat these procedures twice more at points 4 and 5 to form the last two fingers.

    f. Reenter at the last exit point and push the needle through the hand to point 1. Exit at 1 and lock the stitch. Do not cut the thread.

  7. Position the arms at shoulder level and whipstitch them to the body securely.

  8. For one shoe, place two Shoe pieces right sides together and stitch the seam along the long curved edge, leaving the straight upper edge open and unstitched (**Figure G**). Turn the shoe right side out and press a ¼-inch hem allowance to the inside around the raw upper edge. Repeat these procedures to make another shoe.

  9. The legs are made from the ribbed half of the sock that was cut in step 4. Cut this ribbed section in half lengthwise. Fold each half in half again lengthwise, placing right sides together. On each one, stitch the seam along the long edge, leaving both short edges open and unstitched. You should now have two long tubes, with open ends. Turn the leg tubes right side out.

  10. Insert the ribbed end of one leg into the top of one shoe, aligning the leg seam with the center back shoe seam (**Figure H**). Whipstitch the leg and shoe together. Stuff the leg and shoe through the open leg end with the fiberfill, stopping about ½ inch from the open end. The leg should be about 5 inches in circumference. Repeat these procedures to form another leg.

MORE GREAT PANTYHOSE CRAFTS

Figure I

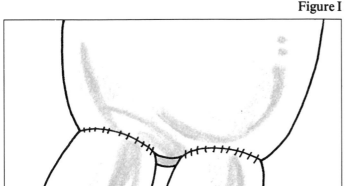

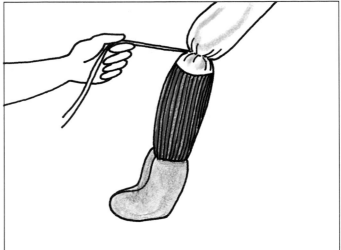

11. To attach the legs to the body, first press a ½-inch hem allowance to the inside around the open lower edge of the torso. Insert the open upper ends of the legs (**Figure I**), and whipstitch the legs to the body.

12. Tie off a knee (or stitch back and forth through the leg) about 1 inch above the ribbed part of the leg (**Figure J**). The contrasting color of the ribbed portion should look like the doll's knee sock.

Adding the Facial Features

1. Use a long sharp needle and one continuous length of heavy-duty thread (approximately 20 inches) for the entire procedure. Follow the entry and exit points illustrated in **Figure K**.

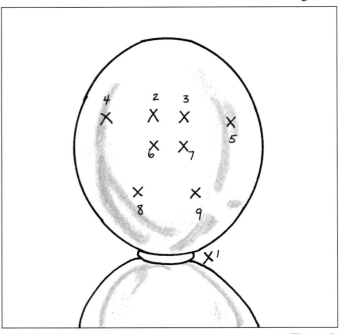

   a. To form the bridge of the nose, enter at 1 (the back of the neck), and exit at 2.
   b. Reenter at 2 and exit at 3.
   c. Reenter at 3 and exit at 2. Gently pull the thread to form the bridge of the nose, take another stitch back and forth underneath the surface between 2 and 3 to secure the nose, and exit at 2.
   d. To form the eye lines, pull the thread across the surface, enter at 4, and exit at 3.
   e. Pull the thread across the surface, enter at 5, and exit at point 2.
   f. Gently pull the thread until the eye lines appear, lock the stitch, and exit at 3.
   g. To form the nose, reenter at 3 and exit at 6.
   h. Pull the thread across the surface, enter at 7, and exit at 2. Pull the thread until a small nose appears. Lock the stitch and exit at 3.
   i. To form the mouth, reenter at 3 and exit at 8.
   j. Pull the thread across the surface, enter at 9, and exit at 2. Gently pull the thread until a smile appears, then lock the stitch at 2.
   k. Reenter at 2 and exit at 1. Lock the stitch and then cut the thread.

2. Glue a button to the center of each eye line. We drew a small black pupil in the center of each eye button, using a black felt-tip pen.

3. Brush a little cosmetic cheek blusher across the doll's cheeks and bottom lip. Use the brown eyebrow pencil to draw

Figure L

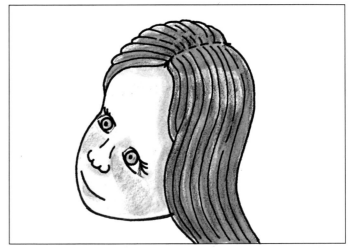

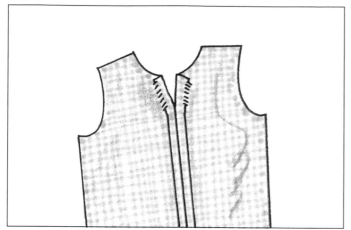

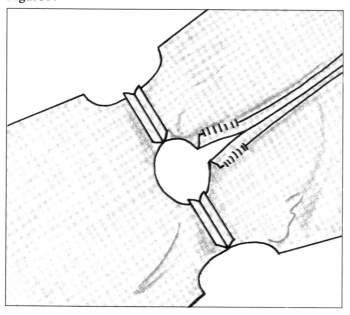

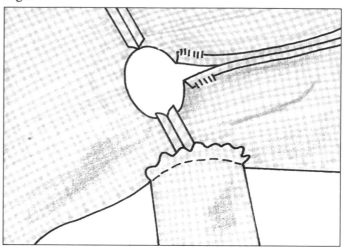

eyebrows above the button eyes and to dot freckles across the nose and cheeks. We also drew eyelashes above Portia's eyes.

Making the Hair

Note: Use half of the skein of rug yarn for each doll's hair.

1. To make Portia's hair, cut the yarn into 24-inch lengths and place them across the top of her head (**Figure L**). Stitch the yarn to the head to form a center part using a backstitch.

2. On each side of Portia's head, gather the yarn into a pigtail even with the mouth line. Tie the pigtail using a length of heavy-duty thread, and stitch the tied portion to her head. Glue the yarn to her head between the center part and the tied portion of the pigtail. Wrap a length of blue ribbon around each pigtail to cover the thread, and tie it in a bow at the front.

3. To make Skipper's hair, cut the yarn into 14-inch lengths and stitch it to his head in the same manner as you did Portia's. Spread the yarn evenly in all directions and trim it to form bangs, sides, and back. You can glue the yarn to his head in several places to help hold it in place.

Making Portia's Dress

Note: All seam allowances are $\frac{3}{8}$ inch unless otherwise specified in the instructions.

1. Transfer all of the placement circles from the patterns to the fabric.

2. Place the two Dress Back pieces right sides together and stitch the center back seam from the lower edge to the small circle. Leave the upper portion of the seam open and unstitched. Press the seam open. Press the seam allowances to the wrong side of the fabric along the upper (unstitched) portion of the seam and whipstitch them in place (**Figure M**).

3. Place the Dress Front and Dress Back assembly right sides together, matching shoulder edges. Stitch the shoulder seams and press them open (**Figure N**).

4. Gather the upper edge of one Sleeve $\frac{3}{8}$ inch from the raw edge between the small circles. Place the Sleeve and dress right sides together, matching armhole edges, and adjust the gathers evenly. Stitch along the gathering line, as shown in **Figure O**. Attach the remaining Sleeve to the opposite side of the dress in the same manner.

5. Fold the dress right sides together and stitch the underarm and side seams on each side (**Figure P**).

6. To create the ruffle you will need a length of gingham 3 x 50 inches. Cut several long gingham rectangles that are 3 inches wide, and piece them together end to end to form one 50-inch-long strip.

7. Press a $\frac{1}{4}$-inch hem allowance to the wrong side of the fabric along one long edge of the Ruffle. Stitch the hem in place.

8. Fold the Ruffle in half widthwise, right sides together. Stitch a seam across the short end and press it open. You should now have one continuous strip. Run a line of basting stitches $\frac{1}{4}$ inch from the long raw edge, and another $\frac{1}{2}$ inch from the edge. Pull up the basting threads to form even gathers until the strip measures the same as the circumference of the lower edge of the dress.

9. A row of eyelet trim is attached between the lower dress edge and the top of the Ruffle at the seam line. Pin a length of eyelet trim around the lower dress edge with right sides together. The bound edge of the eyelet should be even with the

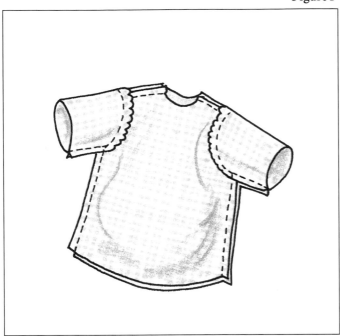

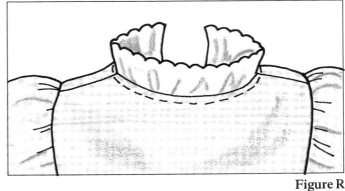

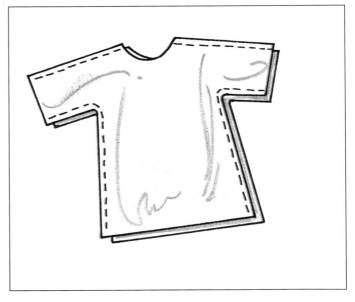

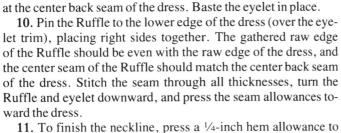

raw edge of the dress, and the scalloped edge should extend up toward the top of the dress. Turn back the raw ends of the eyelet at the center back seam of the dress. Baste the eyelet in place.

10. Pin the Ruffle to the lower edge of the dress (over the eyelet trim), placing right sides together. The gathered raw edge of the Ruffle should be even with the raw edge of the dress, and the center seam of the Ruffle should match the center back seam of the dress. Stitch the seam through all thicknesses, turn the Ruffle and eyelet downward, and press the seam allowances toward the dress.

11. To finish the neckline, press a ¼-inch hem allowance to the wrong side of the fabric all the way around the edge. Stitch a length of eyelet trim along the pressed edge so that the scalloped edge of the eyelet extends upward, forming a stand-up collar (**Figure Q**).

12. The lower edge of each sleeve can be fitted to Portia's wrist in one of two ways: The easiest way is to press a narrow hem to the wrong side of the fabric, stitch a length of eyelet trim around the sleeve hem, and then gather the end of the sleeve using a running stitch. If you prefer, you can make a casing to accommodate elastic at the end of each sleeve. To make a casing, first press a narrow hem to the wrong side of the fabric. Press a second ½-inch-wide hem to the wrong side and stitch close to the edge, leaving a small opening to accommodate the elastic. Run a second stitching line ¼ inch from the first one to form the casing (**Figure R**). Topstitch a length of eyelet trim around the end of the sleeve, being careful not to stitch through the casing. Measure Portia's wrist and cut a piece of elastic ½ inch longer. Thread the elastic through the sleeve casing. Stitch the ends of the elastic securely together and then pull it back inside the casing. Whipstitch the opening in the casing. Repeat these procedures to finish the lower end of the other sleeve. Attach a hook and eye closure to the top of the neck opening of the dress.

Making Skipper's Clothing

1. Place the two Shirt pieces right sides together and stitch the shoulder and side seams on each side (**Figure S**). Turn the shirt right side out.

2. Skipper's shirt has ribbing at the ends of the sleeves and around the neckline. For each sleeve cut a rectangle from the blue ribbing fabric, 1½ inch wide and 1 inch longer than the

Figure T

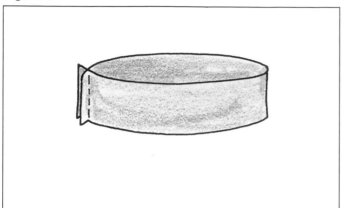

Figure U

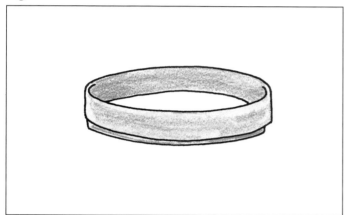

Figure V

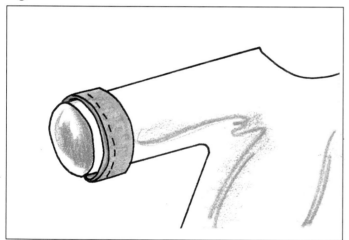

Figure W

Figure X

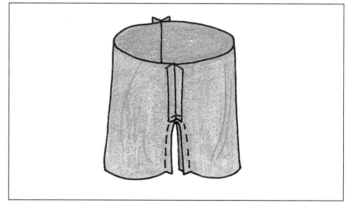

measurement around Skipper's arm just above the elbow. For the neckline, cut a similar ribbing rectangle, 1½ inches wide and 1 inch longer than the measurement around his neck. For each of these pieces, the ribbing lines should run widthwise across the strip, not lengthwise.

3. Fold one of the sleeve ribbing pieces in half widthwise, placing right sides together, and stitch a ½-inch seam across the short edges (**Figure T**). The piece is now a continuous cylinder. Fold down one raw edge of the cylinder until it is even with the opposite raw edge, placing the wrong sides together, as shown in **Figure U**. The seam allowances should be on the inside now. Pin the long raw edges together. Repeat these procedures for the remaining sleeve ribbing piece and for the neckline ribbing piece.

4. Slip one of the sleeve ribbing pieces over the end of one shirt sleeve so that all raw edges are even and the folded edge of the ribbing extends up toward the shoulder (**Figure V**). The seam in the ribbing piece should match the underarm seam of the shirt. Ease the ribbing to fit the opening and stitch the seam ½ inch from the raw edges. Trim the seam allowance to ¼ inch, press the ribbing outward, and press the seam allowances toward the shirt. Repeat these procedures to attach the remaining sleeve ribbing piece and the neckline ribbing piece.

5. Place the two Knicker pieces right sides together and stitch the center front and back seams (**Figure W**).

6. Refold the knickers right sides together, matching the center front and back seams. Stitch the inner leg seam (**Figure X**).

7. Make elastic casings at the waist and leg openings in the same manner as you did on Portia's dress sleeves. Cut the elastic to fit Skipper's waist and legs.

Materials

For the doll:

One leg of regular-weave flesh-tone pantyhose for the head
One pair of off-white tights for the body
A bag of polyester fiberfill
Two skeins of light ivory rug yarn
Four ⅜-inch-diameter flat buttons
Heavy-duty white thread and a long sharp needle
Cosmetic cheek blusher
Acrylic paints in red and brown and a fine-tipped artist's brush,
    or fine-point felt-tip markers in the same colors

For the gown:

1 yard of 45-inch-wide sheer white linen cotton (handkerchief
    or blouse weight)
1½ yards of 2-inch-wide flat finishing lace
2 yards of 1-inch-wide white gathered lace trim
Two snaps, buttons, or ties; and four baby buttons
½ yard of 4-inch-wide gathered white eyelet trim
½ yard of 1-inch-wide white satin ribbon

Cutting the Pieces

1. Scale drawings for the Body, Arm, Leg, Sleeve, Back Yoke, and Front Yoke are provided in **Figure A**. Enlarge the drawings to make full-size patterns.

2. Cut both legs from the white tights at the panty line. Cut the toe portion from each leg, and slit each leg lengthwise so you have two large flat rectangles of material.

3. Cut the pieces listed in this step from the specified fabrics.

Off-white tights fabric: Body – cut two
                         Arm – cut four
                         Leg – cut four
White linen: Front Yoke – cut one
             Back Yoke – cut two
             Sleeve – cut two
             Skirt – cut two, each 14 x 45 inches

Making the Head

1. Tie a knot just below the panty line in one leg of pantyhose. Cut across the hose about 1 inch above the knot, and again about 10 inches below the knot. Turn the hose so the knot is on the inside, and stuff with fiberfill until the head is approximately 5½ inches in diameter. Tie the hose in a knot at the neck.

2. To sculpt the facial features, use heavy-duty flesh-tone thread and a long sharp needle, and follow the entry and exit points illustrated in **Figure B**.

   a. Enter at 1 and exit at 2. To form the nose, sew a circle of basting stitches about the size of a quarter, and exit at point 3.

   b. Use the tip of the needle to very carefully lift the fiberfill within the circle. Gently pull the thread until the little round nose appears. Lock the stitch and exit at 2.

   c. To form the nostrils, reenter at 2 and exit at 4.

   d. Enter ¼ inch above 4 and exit at 3.

Priscilla Doll

Here's an adorable little lady who is guaranteed to charm doll lovers of all ages. Her fancy christening gown also will fit a small infant, or can easily be altered to fit a larger child. Priscilla is about 20 inches tall.

   e. Reenter at 3 and exit at 5.

   f. Enter about ¼ inch above 5 and exit at 2. Pull the thread and lock the stitch at 2.

   g. To form the eye lines, pull the thread across the surface, enter at 6, and exit at 3.

   h. Pull the thread across the surface, enter at 7, and exit at 2. Pull the thread gently to form the eye lines, and lock the stitch at 2.

   i. To form the mouth, reenter at 2 and exit at 8.

   j. Pull the thread across the surface, enter at 9, and exit at 10. Pull the thread across the surface, enter at 9, and exit at 2. Pull the thread until a smile appears. Lock the stitch at point 2.

   k. To form a dimple, reenter at 2 and exit at 11. Reenter at 11 and exit at 2. Pull the thread until a dimple appears, and lock the stitch at 2.

   l. To form the second dimple, reenter at 2 and exit at 12. Reenter at 12 and exit at 2. Pull the thread until the second dimple appears, and lock the stitch at 2. Reenter at 2, exit at 1, lock the stitch, and cut the thread.

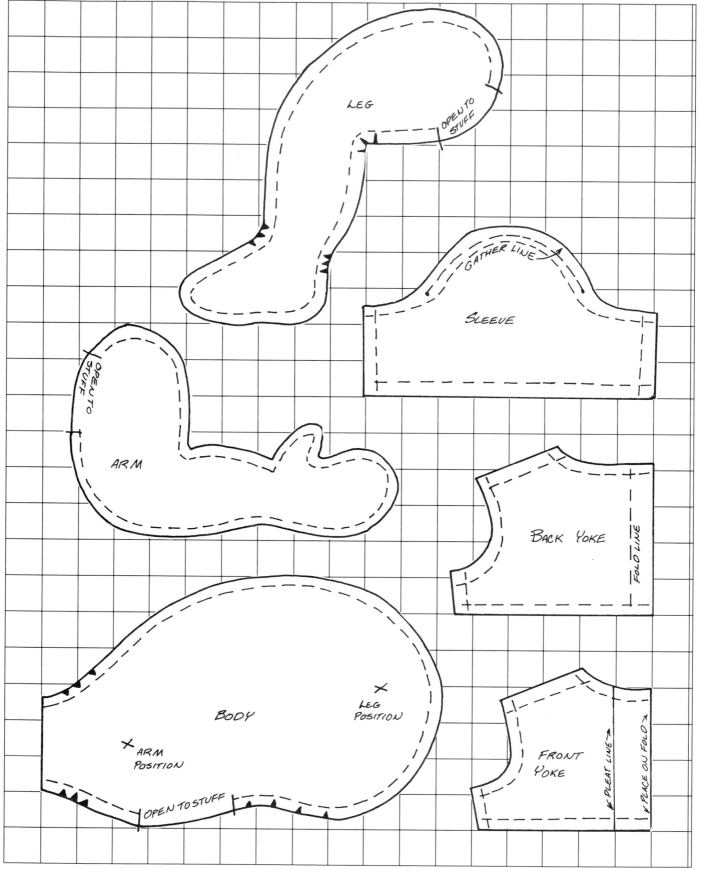

LEG

OPEN TO STUFF

GATHER LINE

SLEEVE

OPEN TO STUFF

ARM

BACK YOKE

FOLD LINE

BODY

LEG POSITION

ARM POSITION

OPEN TO STUFF

FRONT YOKE

PLEAT LINE

PLACE ON FOLD

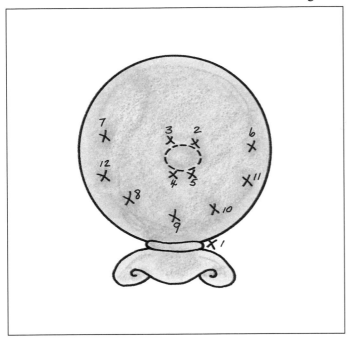

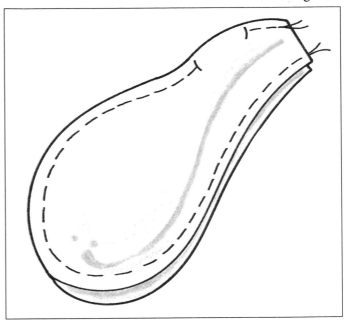

3. Brush a little cosmetic blusher across Priscilla's cheeks and nose.

4. Use the brown felt-tip marker or acrylic paint to draw the eyelashes and eyebrows; and use the red marker or paint to color in the lips.

Making the Body, Arms, and Legs

1. Pin the two Body pieces right sides together and stitch the seam as shown in **Figure C**, leaving the neck edge open and leaving an opening in the back seam as shown. (Placement of the back opening is indicated on the scale drawing of the Body piece.) Be sure to use a zigzag setting or stretch-stitch on your machine, so the thread will not break when the body is stuffed and stretched slightly. Turn the body right side out, but do not stuff it just yet. Turn a narrow allowance to the inside of the body around the open neck edge.

2. To attach the head, slip the tied neck portion through the open neck edge of the body, aligning the front body seam with the center of the face. Work through the opening at the back of the body to whipstitch around the neck several times, to secure the head.

3. Stuff the body with fiberfill through the back opening. Turn the seam allowances to the inside along the opening, and then whipstitch the opening edges together.

4. Place two Arm pieces right sides together and stitch the seam, as shown in **Figure D**, leaving an opening near the shoulder. Turn the arm right side out and stuff it with fiberfill.

5. Make a second arm in the same manner, using the two remaining Arm pieces.

6. Place two Leg pieces right sides together and stitch the seam, as shown in **Figure E**, leaving an opening near the upper end. Turn the leg right side out and stuff.

7. Make a second leg in the same manner, using the two remaining Leg pieces.

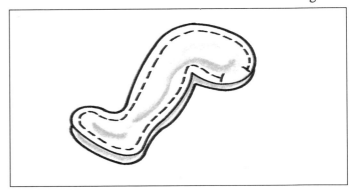

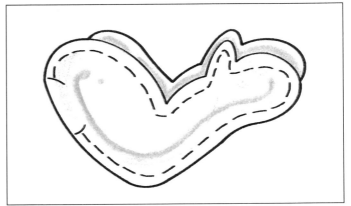

Sculpting the Arms and Legs

1. To sculpt and reinforce the elbows, use heavy-duty thread and follow the entry and exit points illustrated in **Figure F**.

    a. Enter at point 1 on one side of the arm, push the needle straight through the arm, and exit directly opposite 1 on the other side.

Figure F

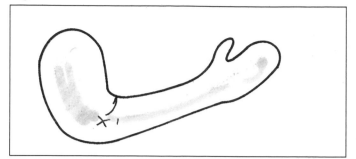

Figure G

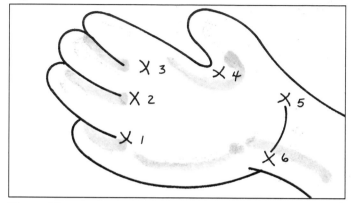

Figure H

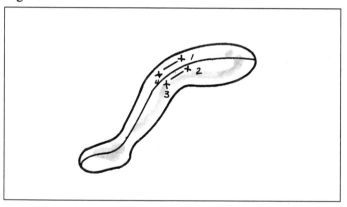

Figure I

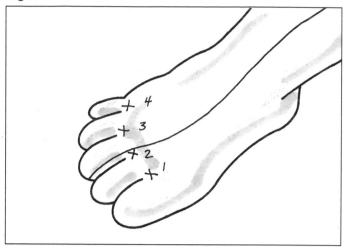

d. Repeat steps b and c at point 2 and then at point 3 to form the remaining fingers. When you have completed the steps at point 3, lock the stitch securely at point 3 on the palm side, but do not cut the thread.

e. To give Priscilla a wrist, reenter at 3 on the palm and exit at 4 on the palm. Reenter at 4 and exit at 5 on the palm side. Pull the thread across the surface, enter at 6, and exit at 4 on the palm. Gently pull the thread until the wrist and palm appear, then lock the stitch at 4 and cut the thread.

f. Repeat the procedures described in steps a through e to sculpt the other hand. Be sure to use the opposite side of the second hand as the palm, so the hands are mirror images of each other.

3. To sculpt Priscilla's knees, follow the entry and exit points illustrated in **Figure H**.

a. Enter at point 1 on one side of the front leg seam, push the needle straight through the knee, and exit at 2 on the other side of the front leg seam.

b. Pull the thread across the surface and enter at 3. Push the needle straight through the knee and exit at 4.

c. Pull the thread across the surface and enter at 1.

d. Repeat the procedures in steps a through c to reinforce the knee. Lock the stitch at 1 but do not cut the thread.

e. To sculpt the back of the knee, reenter at 1 and exit on the same side of the leg, just at the knee bend. Pull the thread across the surface, around the back of the knee, and enter opposite the previous exit point. Push the needle straight through the leg and lock the stitch.

f. Repeat the procedures in steps a through e to sculpt the knee on the other leg.

4. To sculpt the toes, follow the entry and exit points illustrated in **Figure I**.

a. To form the base of the big toe, enter at point 1 on the sole, and exit directly opposite 1 on the top of the foot.

b. Wrap the thread around the end of the foot as shown, and reenter at 1 on the sole. Exit at 1 on the top of the the foot. Pull the thread tightly to form the big toe, and lock the stitch by taking a very small stitch at 1, exiting on the top of the foot.

b. Pull the thread across the surface at the bend of the elbow, as shown, enter at 1, and exit opposite 1.

c. Lock the stitch at 1 and cut the thread.

d. Repeat the procedures in steps a through c to sculpt the elbow on the other arm.

2. To sculpt the fingers, follow the entry and exit points illustrated in **Figure G**, using heavy-duty white thread and a long sharp needle.

a. To form the base of the pinky finger, enter at point 1 on the palm, and exit directly opposite point 1 on the back of the hand.

b. Wrap the thread around the end of the hand as shown, and enter at 1 on the palm. Exit at 1 on the back of hand. Pull the thread tightly to form the first finger, and lock the stitch by taking another very small stitch at 1.

c. To form the base of the ring finger, reenter at 1 and exit at 2 on the back of the hand.

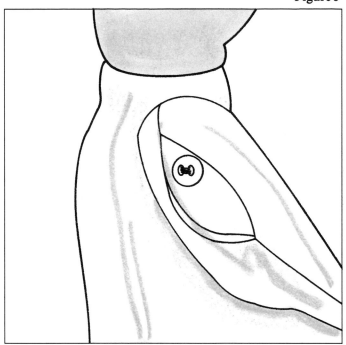

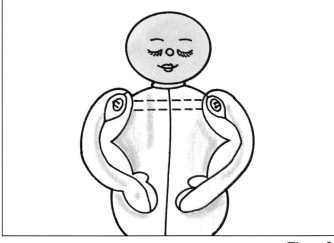

Figure L

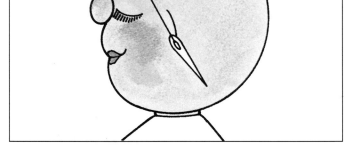

c. To form the second toe, reenter at 1, push the needle underneath the surface, and exit at 2 on the top of the foot.

d. Repeat steps b and c at point 2, then at point 3, and then at point 4 to form the remaining toes. When you have completed the steps at point 4, lock the stitch securely and cut the thread.

e. Repeat the procedures described in steps a through d to sculpt the toes on the other foot. Be sure to make the second foot a mirror image of the first one.

Assembling the Body

The arms and legs are sewn to the body so that they can move as if jointed. The thread is secured to a button located inside each arm and leg.

1. Work through the opening near the shoulder to stitch one of the flat buttons to the inside of one arm, as shown in **Figure J**. Be sure to sew the button to the side of the arm that will face the body, which is the same as the palm side of the hand. Stitch a button to the inside of the other arm in the same manner.

2. Use the long sharp needle and heavy-duty thread to attach the arms to the body. To begin, place an arm on each side of the body, as shown in **Figures J** and **K**; the palms should face inward. Work through the opening near each shoulder to stitch back and forth several times through the body and arm buttons, as shown in **Figure K**. Pull the thread gently as you work so that the arms are pulled snugly against the body, but not so snugly that they will not move. Lock the final stitch inside one arm and cut the thread.

3. Add a little more fiberfill inside the shoulder area of each arm. Turn the opening edges to the inside of each arm and whipstitch them together.

4. Work through the opening near the top of one leg to stitch a flat button to the inside of the leg. Be sure that the button is sewn to the side of the leg that includes the big toe. Stitch a button to the inside of the other leg in the same manner.

5. Placement marks for the legs are provided on the scale drawing of the Body pattern. Place a leg against each side of the body, aligning the buttons inside the legs with the placement marks on the Body pattern. Be sure that you have the correct leg on each side (big toes at the center), and stitch the legs in place using the same procedures as you did to attach the arms.

Adding the Hair

1. The ivory-colored yarn is wrapped into curls and sewn to the head. Thread a needle with a generous length of heavy-duty thread, and unwrap one of the skeins of yarn. Tack one end of the yarn to the front of Priscilla's head at the center of the hairline. Do not cut the thread, as you will be working with it to tack the curls in place. For the time being, stick the needle into the head near the tacked yarn.

2. To make one curl, wrap the yarn tightly around a pencil approximately twenty times. Insert the threaded needle between the yarn loops and the pencil, and pull it out the opposite end. Remove the yarn from the pencil while holding the loops together, and tack the yarn curl to the head over the original tacked end of the yarn (**Figure L**).

Figure M

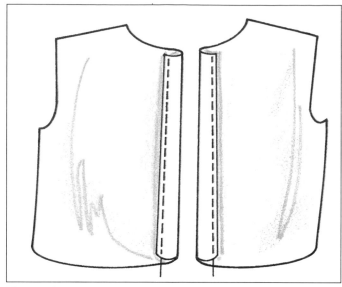

Figure N

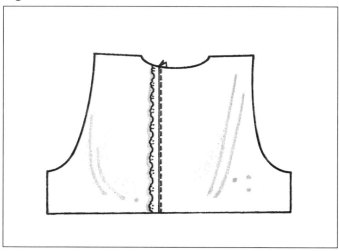

Figure O

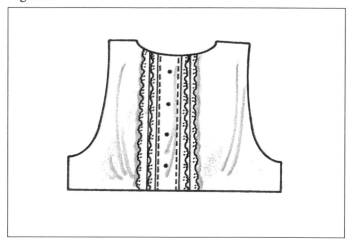

3. Repeat the procedures described in step 2 until the head is completely covered with curls. When the thread becomes too short, lock the stitch and rethread the needle. Use both skeins of yarn, if necessary.

4. When the last curl is in place, lock the stitch. Cut the yarn and tack the end underneath a curl.

Making the Gown Yoke

1. To prepare each Back Yoke piece, press a ½-inch-wide hem to the wrong side of the fabric along the center back edge (**Figure M**). Topstitch each of these hems as shown.

2. The Front Yoke will contain two vertical pleats, with a length of lace sewn into each one (**Figure N**). To form the pleat on one side of the Front Yoke, fold the fabric right sides together along the pleat line indicated on the pattern, and pin the layers together about ¼ inch from the fold. Cut a length of 1-inch-wide gathered lace trim to match the length of the pleat and insert the bound edge of the lace between the layers of the pleat, removing and replacing the pins to hold the lace in place. Fold the pleat toward the center of the Yoke, as shown in **Figure N**. Move the

pins to the right side of the fabric. Topstitch along the pleat on the right side of the fabric, sewing through all thicknesses, as shown in **Figure N**.

3. Stitch an identical pleat, with lace trim, on the opposite side of the vertical center line of the Yoke Front.

4. Cut two additional lengths of lace trim and topstitch these lengths to the Yoke Front, just outside each of the pleats, as shown in **Figure O**. Sew the baby buttons to the vertical center line of the Yoke Front, as shown.

5. Pin one Back Yoke piece to the Front Yoke along the shoulder edge, placing right sides together. Repeat for the other Back Yoke piece. Stitch the shoulder seam on each side, and press each of these seams open.

6. Press a narrow hem to the wrong side of the fabric along the straight lower edge of one Sleeve piece. Cut a length of gathered lace trim to match the length of the lower Sleeve edge, and pin the bound edge of the lace to the wrong side of the Sleeve edge. The scalloped edge of the lace should extend out beyond the sleeve. Topstitch along the pressed edge to secure the hem and lace. Hem and trim the lower edge of the remaining Sleeve piece in the same manner.

7. Run a line of basting stitches along the curved upper edge of each Sleeve piece, as indicated by the gathering line provided on the Sleeve pattern. Do not cut the tails of thread.

8. Pin the basted edge of one sleeve to the armhole edge at one side of the yoke assembly, placing right sides together and pulling the basting threads to gather the sleeve to fit. Adjust the gathers evenly and stitch the seam, as shown in **Figure P**. Stitch the remaining sleeve to the armhole edge at the opposite side of the yoke assembly in the same manner. Press the seam allowances toward the dress.

9. Fold the yoke and sleeve assembly right sides together and stitch the underarm and side seam on each side. Press the seams open. Run a line of basting stitches around each sleeve, about ½ inch from the lace-trimmed lower edge. Do not cut the tails of thread, as the sleeves will be gathered around the arms later.

Adding the Skirt

1. One of the Skirt pieces will serve as the Outer Skirt and the other will serve as the Underskirt. Press and stitch a ¼-inch-wide hem to the wrong side of the fabric along one long edge

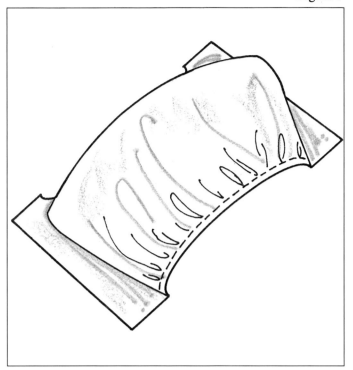

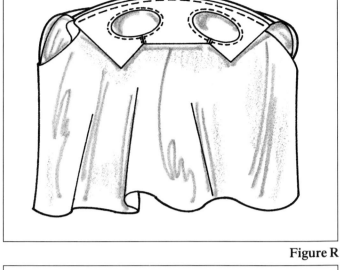

of each Skirt piece. These will be the lower edges. Press and stitch a 1-inch-wide hem to the wrong side of the fabric along both short edges of each Skirt piece. These will be the back opening edges. Stack the two Skirt pieces evenly, placing both of them right side up. Be sure that each is turned the same way end for end, so the lower edges are aligned and the upper edges are aligned. Run a line of basting stitches through both layers, close to the aligned upper edges. This edge will be gathered to fit the gown yoke, so do not cut off the trails of thread.

2. Pull up the basting threads to gather the upper edge of the skirt assembly, so that it is the same length as the lower edge of the yoke assembly. Tie off the threads, adjust the gathers evenly, and baste over them to hold them in place.

3. Place the gathered skirt assembly right side up on a flat surface. Cut a length of gathered lace trim to match the length of the gathered upper edge of the skirt. Pin the lace to the skirt, placing the bound edge of the lace along the gathered edge of the skirt. The scalloped edge of the lace should extend toward the lower edge of the skirt. Baste the lace in place close to the bound edge.

4. Place the skirt and yoke assemblies right sides together, aligning the upper edge of the skirt with the lower edge of the yoke. The lace will be sandwiched between the skirt and yoke. Stitch the seam, as shown in **Figure Q**, turn the skirt downward, and press the seam allowances toward the yoke.

5. To finish the neckline, press a narrow hem to the wrong side of the fabric and topstitch a length of gathered lace trim to the pressed edge, as you did for the sleeves. Turn the ends of the lace to the wrong side.

6. To finish the lower edge of the skirt, turn and press a narrow hem to the wrong side of the fabric along the lower edge of the Outer Skirt and along the lower edge of the Underskirt.

Topstitch 2-inch-wide flat finishing lace around the bottom of the Outer Skirt, and topstitch gathered lace trim around the bottom of the Underskirt.

7. Priscilla is probably a little chilly by now, so dress her in her gown. Pull up the basting threads around the lower edge of each sleeve to gather the sleeve around the arm, and tie off the threads. Sew the snaps, buttons, or ties to the upper corners of the back yoke opening, and secure them together. If you wish, use a piece of white scrap fabric and a couple of safety pins to diaper Priscilla.

8. To create the bonnet, glue or tack the length of 4-inch-wide eyelet trim to Priscilla's head, as shown in **Figure R**. Cut the 1-inch-wide ribbon in half, and tack one end of each length underneath the bonnet, on opposite sides. Tie the ribbons in a bow under her chin.

About the Family...

The Family Workshop, a one-of-a-kind creative idea company, is located in Bixby, Oklahoma. The company specializes in the field of how-to, with subjects ranging from fabric crafts and woodworking to home improvement, photography, and personal computers.

The Family Workshop originated, quite literally, on the Baldwins' front porch. Ed and Stevie, long-time hobbyists and experts in the do-it-yourself field, began writing a newspaper column called "Makin' Things." Since 1977, the family has grown to include other craftspersons, woodworkers, artists, and editors, who have helped provide the public with do-it-yourself tips, pointers, and projects through television programs, syndicated columns, quarterly newsletters, and a series of books for a number of major publishing houses.

Ed and Stevie, nationally known and respected how-to newspaper columnists, appeared in over 100 segments of a TV series that provided viewers time- and money-saving ideas for making things at home.

This energetic couple also has done a number of product promotions for major companies in the do-it-yourself field, as well as appearing in various TV commercials. They have been featured in training films and demonstrations for several different major organizations.

Since the birth of the company, the Baldwins and their staff have authored and produced more than a dozen how-to books. These publications include subjects such as family computers, furniture building, and making projects from fabric scraps. Impressively, nine of the books have been either main, featured alternate, or alternate selections for either the Better Homes & Gardens or Popular Science book clubs.

The Family Workshop currently produces three syndicated weekly newspaper columns. The original craft-oriented column, "Makin' Things," was first written and produced in 1975. Since that time, Ed and Stevie and their staff have created two additional columns: "The Woodwright," and "Kid's Stuff." The three columns appear weekly in publications with a combined readership of over 26 million. "Classified Crafts," their most recent newspaper service, was started in 1983. The Family Workshop's newspaper features run in more than 500 daily and weekly newspapers across the country, with more than 750 appearances per week.